AFRAID TO BE FREE

JEANNETTE L. ROWE

ARCHER-ELLISON PUBLISHING

WINTER PARK, FLORIDA

ARCHER-ELLISON PUBLISHING
P.O. BOX 5795
WINTER PARK. FLORIDA 32792

DESIGNED BY KIMBERLY D'ANGELO

MANUFACTURED IN THE UNITED STATES OF AMERICA

ISBN 1-57472-300-6

ACKNOWLEDGEMENTS

To my husband: Thank you Jack Wayne Rowe, Jr., for the many hours of patience, warmth, support and encouragement that made writing this book possible. And thank you for allowing me to be free.

To my children: Thank you Rick Davis, Susan Kelleher and Joey Theiss for growing with me, blossoming in spite of my mistakes, and allowing me draw on your life-experiences for many of these writings. Rick, thank you for being my wisest spiritual counselor. Susan, thank you for inciting me to riot, for giving me my first granddaughter and for all the inner joy and pain only a mother and daughter can share. Joey, thank you for that special unconditional love and respect you impart to me.

To my father (now deceased) and mother: Thank you, Louis and Louise Owens, for teaching me the value of liberty and inspiring me to be free.

To my sisters: Thank you Barbara Jean Gregory and Nancy Lynn Bigley for the enrichments you've added to my life.

To my friends: Thank you Charles and Joann Ginn, for prodding me to turn these written pages into a real book.

To my favorite instructor: Thank you Kathleen R. Lockney, (MDE) for proof-reading every page, correcting all my grammar and encouraging me to print every word I wrote. But most of all, thank you for being an inspiration to my son throughout his high school years.

Contents

Introduction 1

1: From The Shadows
   Of The Silent Majority 5

2: Fallout From A Fake Utopia 13

3: Racism Be Gone 21

4: Ebonics - Another Language Barrier 27

5: More Reverse Discrimination 33

6: Remembering Foreign Policy 47

7: Who's Who In America 55

8: Badgering Bad Agents 63

9: Take Back Control Of Your Kids 71

10: Take Back Control Of Your Schools........ 87

11: Call Out The Press 103

12: Reclaim Your Land 115

13: Put A Moratorium On Regulations 121

14: Illegal Search And Seizure 129

15: Deregulate The Innocent 133

16: Revamp The Justice System..................... 137

17: It's Time Crime Didn't Pay 143

18: Ending Government's
    Bad Business Practices 149

Index: 161

Introduction

My Mother rocked and warmed me by an old wood stove. My early childhood was spent trekking around the countryside or fishing with my Dad along the banks of the Ohio River. Two good legs were the only mode of transportation back then. We were poor and there were no amenities - like indoor plumbing or electricity. When I got old enough, I started reading by the light of an oil lamp and traipsing to the outhouse through the snow. By five I had two little sisters and was helping to raise the food they ate.

In my neck of the woods, freedom and thought were reserved for men and emotions belonged only to women. But I was a tomboy-agitator who never quite learned my rightful place. I scribbled profound thoughts on tablets of stone, and then insisted that my Dad read them. Just as I was entering high school and evolving into a rebellious teenager my family moved to a town in northern Ohio. I quit school in my senior year. By the time I was twenty-one I'd been married, had a child, divorced, and remarried - but I still hadn't found my rightful place.

I went back to school for my Graduate Equivalent Diploma (GED) and had two more children before I was twenty-five. My second husband was domineering to say the least, and the marriage was violent most of the time. But my mission in life was finally clear - liberate myself to raise my children to be the best they could be. I cared for the kids, dabbled at odd jobs, took some college courses, and jotted down solutions to the world's problems in between trying to solve my own.

With another divorce, a third husband, eleven hundred dollars, everything we owned in a suitcase, and the kids tucked under my belt, I headed for Florida to start anew.

Times were tough and the road was poor and rocky, but I was succeeding. The new marriage was a little better and the kids were doing great - excellent grades, good friends, and the highest honors all through high school. I became a real estate broker and instructor and my husband followed. Together we built our own business, developed land, and saw all three kids finish college.

Today I own over 600 acres of land, drive a new Lincoln Town Car with a built-in telephone, play with three beautiful grandchildren, carry an electronic notebook everywhere I go, and I'm working toward my final goal - preserving this better world for my children and yours. I guess you could say I've seen and adapted to change, even when it was frightening and unwelcome.

But only one change frightens me today. And it is not speed nor high tech equipment. It isn't even crime or the lack of morals. It is our indifference toward liberty, and the lack of freedom we Americans tolerate. We seem to have forgotten that as the rights of the majority go, so go the rights of everybody else in the country.

When the majority loses individual freedoms, nobody is free. When the rights of criminals take priority over law abiding citizens, nobody is safe. When the majority forfeits their private property rights, the land of the free is not preserved. When free enterprise succumbs to government control, the masses no longer prosper. When taxes and administrative costs bankrupt the majority, the whole nation lives in poverty. When the majority is taught and indoctrinated by the state, the children are left uneducated and liberty is misunderstood. When the majority does not speak out, the voice of the people is not heard. And when the majority does not stand up for the cause of freedom, democracy fades away.

We older Americans were freedom born and bred. But we've allowed a gluttonous government to sidetrack us with fear, and some book-peddling psychologists to render our hearts and minds indifferent to it. We've passed that fear down to the generations that have followed us. Today our citizens are afraid to buck the government, afraid to punish criminals, afraid to stand up to and for their kids. Young parents are so afraid they won't have enough money to last through the next paycheck, let alone retirement, that they can't stop working - even when their own children need them at home. And we're all afraid of each other. In fact, we're so afraid that we don't even trust our own good judgement any more.

But we can and we must overcome this apprehension that drains our power to reason and zaps our common sense. For only as our misguided fears dissipate will the courage of freedom ring throughout our land again. Only when our minds and souls are liberated will we have the decision-making strength necessary to restore law and order to America - and the faster we bring on that change, the better.

As I wrote these words, there were times when even I had to fight the urge to turn away. If you are so inclined, or overwhelmed with the lengthy problems, do not flounder in fear and frustration - just skip to the solutions and go to work on them. For as we come together, exchanging today's fearful fallout for some reality and common sense, America will be set free again. And the whole world will surely follow.

At times my writings may offend you, for it is not my intent to be politically correct; it is my intent to stir you and move you toward the fight for freedom. For lack of better examples, I may have portrayed some public figures in a negative light, and even misplaced a few details. But it is my hope that you will focus on and respond to the cry for freedom and truth, rather than on my human frailties. I ask that you ponder my words with a fair and open mind, and reexamine your position in their light, as I have had to do from time to time.

I dedicate this book to my three children and my grandchildren. And I ask that they join with your children and grandchildren to keep ours the land of the free - forever.

From The Shadows Of The Silent Majority

Like most in our area, my father believed men should go to war and work, and rule the roost; that children should be seen and not heard; and that the women of the house should serve him. God and Country was the "in" thing back then. And girls with marketable skills had bad reputations - at least where I came from.

But somewhere, for some strange reason, at some point when I was too young to understand why, I picked up the head-strong notion that I should be liberated. From that moment on, my childhood became one uneasy struggle for freedom after another.

The podium from which I protested was isolated in a wooded hillside along the banks of the Ohio River, and the only audience present at my rallies were family members. Grandpa and Uncle Morris heckled and laughed me off. One sister was busy playing house and the other was too young to care.

Grandma, liberated as she was before her time, refused to discuss any political agenda, but she had her own private way of egging me on. She was an excellent role model - openly defying Grandpa's attempts to dominate her life, and even talking back to him in front of me. She walked five miles each way, just to vote in every election. And she made subtle little comments that, while infuriating Mom, inspired me to keep up the fight. As for my mom, her response to my liberating ideas was always the same - "Don't start again tonight; you'll just upset your dad."

Dad marched staunchly to the beat of an old chauvinistic drum. But as the oldest of three girls, I couldn't resist trying to wear the pants of the son he never had. The harder he tried to keep me in my place in the kitchen, the more like him I became - terribly independent, strongly opinioned, and determined to convince everyone around that I was right. His open confrontations gave me an opportunity to speak out, and a real audience when I did. Although he lectured and contradicted more than he listened, he took my subject matter seriously. And you better believe he provided me a lot of hot feedback.

Daddy was an old World War II veteran who had seen firsthand what government control could do to a country. And he understood that my war against oppression would never be over. He never believed in any giant conspiracy to overtake America, or any other country - not even during McCarthy's Red Scare. Philosophy according to Louis Owens went something like:

"All it takes to conquer the masses is just one little man. And he's always right out in plain sight, indoctrinating and manipulating people into believing his power will make the world a better place. But once in power, that tyrant ravages the land, destroys the democracies, and devastates those who have hailed him onto the throne."

Daddy would slam down my history book and tell me how Japanese suicide missions proved that dictators had little regard for the lives of their loyal subjects. And before I could remind him that World War II was old news, he'd be on to Nazi Germany - "a prime example of just how easily a democracy can fall prey to a single tyrant," he'd bark. "The masses hailed Adolf Hitler into power. And whether out of greed, necessity, or stupidity, the whole world tolerated Hitler's atrocities long enough to be forced into war. Hitler was just one little man, and that was just twenty short years ago", Daddy warned.

Now that I think back on those heated debates, I realize that while I was evolving into a liberal-minded teenager jockeying for position at home, Dad was unwittingly teaching me to value and preserve freedom on a grander scale. And whether the name be Lenin, Stalin, Hitler,

Hirohito, Khrushchev, Castro, or Saddam Hussein, history is still proving Daddy right today.

When Dad saw American liberties begin dissipating at the hands of our federal bureaucracy, he became more and more frightened that America was headed down the wrong path - the path away from freedom. And he overreacted every time he thought something threatened our liberty.

One rainy Sunday afternoon he snapped off the television and called my name. As usual I came running. There he sat - one fist clinched around the other, elbows on his knees. His face grew taut, his throat tightened, and his right foot tapped against the floor as he spoke -"Nikita Khrushchev just pounded his fist and threatened to bury us, right on national television".

I almost died laughing. That was yesterday's news, and I'd seen the replay a dozen times. "Oh come on, Daddy", I goaded. "Khrushchev is a clown with a cherry red nose and mouth. He's a maniac nobody in their right mind takes seriously. They'll never give him the chance to cause international destruction."

"It's no laughing matter", Daddy scolded, as his voice deepened and grew louder. "That little bastard is dangerous. The masses over there have already hailed him into power. And masses here are electing the idiots who'll support his tyranny. He's got enough atomic bombs to destroy half the human race. And by the time he makes his own people miserable, ours will be convinced to intervene. You mark my words, we'll pay dearly to keep that tyrant from strangling freedom," Daddy growled.

Khrushchev the clown, coupled with my dad's ridiculous opinion, was just too funny. I shook my head in disbelief and giggled, just as Mom dropped something on the kitchen floor. The crash was loud enough to let me know that I'd better stop making fun of my father. But before her subtle attempt to alter my attitude had a chance to register, Daddy motioned Mom's way. And we yielded the floor to her dinner call.

We bowed our heads as Mom said grace, but Daddy still had to have the last word. Upon her "Amen," he made sure we all realized that it was he who provided the bread on our table. And when we each had plenty on our plates, he took a portion for himself.

After dinner, Dad retired to the worn-out easy chair he claimed as his own, and we girls did the dishes. "He's Archie Bunker with a hillbilly accent," I whispered to my sister. But by the time the kitchen was clean, he was beginning to sound like the nutty professor - still ranting on about bad dictators. "For centuries, leaders like Hitler and Khrushchev have been scheming to get us to kill each other off" he snarled. "While we live in poverty and die in their bloody battles, they became decorated generals and wealthy kings. They even make us pay taxes to rebuild what their bombs destroy." He rattled off some more foreign historical examples, and insisted that America was going to be next.

I'd heard all these horror stories before. And the thought of fighting wars or becoming a gestapo-type dictatorship scared me half to death. So I tried to reassure myself, and Daddy, that we were wiser, and that the world was more civilized now. "Hitler committed suicide, and Khrushchev is dying," I said, when he paused to catch his breath. "Besides, men can't get away with that kind of barbaric oppression anymore - at least not here."

"You're right," Dad agreed sarcastically. "Nowadays our leaders prefer to tax and regulate us to death. And we've gotten so wise and civilized that we concede our wealth and freedom right here at home, without a fight - and still send our boys off to die in the jungles of Vietnam."

As usual, my attempts to ease his mind only served to further convince him that I had more to learn. Mom, obviously aggravated with another of my fake attempts to lower his blood pressure, scurried off to the kitchen. She hated political discussions. And even though she never moved her lips, I heard her pleading echo through the doorway - "For once, why can't you just agree, instead of arguing with your dad?"

He shook his head in disgust as Mom left the room, and he made some remark about her needing to hear this too, then went right back to talking about too much government control - well, kind of shouting. His words were never soft, nor grammatically correct, but he wasn't about to quiet down until he was convinced that our whole house heard and understood the dangers.

Daddy claimed that climbing interest rates and the soaring price of gas and milk were caused by government's over-regulation of the free enterprise system. He swore up and down that Lyndon Johnson's Great Society was a trend that would ultimately destroy American Democracy. During the Johnson presidency, I got so sick of hearing "You mark my words" that I almost fled to Canada with the draft dodgers. And he shook his finger in my face so many times that I threatened to break it off - under my breath of course. When I scoffed at the notion that America could fall prey to anything resembling socialism, he reminded me that Germany too had been a democracy, and that while Hitler was in the process of creating their great society, Germans had said the same thing.

Sadness radiated from Dad's eyes, and the echo of defeat in his voice worried me. I tried to point out that we were making real social progress under Johnson. But Dad just blew another head gasket. "The man's a socialist," he shouted, "and his wife is worse." I was astounded that my daddy could even think such a thing, let alone say it out loud.

I tried to convince him that the Johnsons were just trying to make the world a better place. "Why Daddy," I said, "Lady Bird is even planting flowers along the freeway." But Dad insisted that those flowers were just part of Johnson's plot to keep ordinary Americans too distracted to notice our freedoms disappearing, and Congress too busy lining their pockets and ballot boxes to intervene on our behalf. "Lady Bird's flowers may make a pretty fragrant landscape, help run up the national debt, and keep the votes coming in while Congress raises taxes," he said, "but they won't cover the graves of our boys dying in southeast Asia, and they won't feed or shelter our needy here at home." No matter what I said, he remained convinced that the Johnsons were among the already rich and powerful, interested in manipulating ordinary people into helping them stay that way. "Only the ignorant and greedy plant flowers while people starve and die," he said, "and the Johnsons aren't ignorant."

I didn't think Daddy had much room to knock the Johnsons. He didn't even give his own kids freedom. Besides, our yard was mostly dirt and weeds, and the dresses we wore on Easter Sunday were made from Grandma's feed sacks. A man that insensitive to beauty at home certainly couldn't appreciate flowers on the freeway. And I can still hear my Mother's gasp when I told him so.

He disguised his tears as smoke-filled eyes, and stamped out his cigarette in a huff. "I quit school and went to work to feed my mother and little brother. In Europe I put my life on the line for this country. I work hard from dusk to dawn to make a living. And you've got some growing up to do before you can even dream of being that free," he grumped. "We may not have much, but I do my best. And you can rest assured that if a hungry stranger comes by, I'll share my last slice of bread - as would any good sensible citizen."

Daddy thought most Americans were, like himself, good decent people with lots of common sense. But I couldn't help but wonder why, with a government by and of and for the people, so many good sensible citizens sat silently by, watching what they believed to be their freedoms going down the tubes. And I just had to ask why he was so proud to be one of them.

Dad just shook his head, and looked the other way. And I remained baffled. He'd always said, "Actions speak louder than words." But when it came to the state of the union, he seemed to be all talk and no action. He'd rant on for hours but never became politically involved. Many times he wished somebody would do something. But he was never sure what, and never considered himself to be the one to do it.

As society begun to deteriorate, I matured into adulthood, and Daddy mellowed with age. His weak heart and my strong one came to agree more and more. We longed for a decent, safe, free society, wherein all the needy were fed. But we knew government would never quite get us there, and we weren't sure who or what would.

Evenings found us sitting sleepily in front of the television, switching through commercials and scanning the preview channel. We'd end up watching nature shows, documentaries, and catching the news at the top of every hour. Before long, we'd both be wide awake and mad - watching every race and creature on earth, except ours, flagrantly and proudly promote the survival of its fittest.

We sat silently by as the government began taking our land for the sake of the environment. Coyotes were encouraged to feed on our cattle. Jungle lions were hailed "noble kings" as they ripped tiny deer to shreds. Even frogs were applauded for jumping up and leaping over to perpetuate the best of their kind, while we were being shamed into forfeiting our land to weeds and snakes. As animal-rights activists chanted of gopher turtle and scrub jay habitats more sacred than our fields of grain, another of our farms was sacrificed to a more endangered species. And nobody mentioned that the world survived on the food we raised and fed them.

As minorities sang sad songs of past hardships, we rushed in to help their poor misguided criminals. As we handed out welfare checks, they burned and looted and killed, and still wreaked havoc in our streets. When they screamed of lack of opportunity, we opened up our neighborhoods and offices. And in the name of equality and fairness, another of our homes was ransacked, another neighbor robbed, another of our daughters raped, and another of our teenagers succumbed to a drug overdose.

As we compromised our values, those demanding that we abolish our moral codes spread AIDS throughout our hospitals. And as they cursed our sacrifice of rats and dogs to research, their sick freely took our medicine.

As we shared new technology with the world, they ruled it more and more illegal for us to prosper. They demanded our jobs and markets, and we gave them up without protest. As we forfeited self advancement to provide opportunity for the disadvantaged, another of our small businesses failed, and the quality of our products plummeted downward.

As we were forced to open our doors and wallets to illegal immigrants, another boat load of foreign outcasts landed on our shores. As we clothed their naked, doctored their sick, and supported their families back home, they held us up with stolen guns and knives.

When crowds screamed of ignorance, we opened our schools to their claims of disadvantage. As the equal rights of promiscuity took priority over quality education and decent moral codes, our best teachers became estranged. Sex education took priority over reading and writing, and our right to pray at school was banned. And while middle class mothers went to work to pay for it all, the greatest nation on earth started falling behind much of the world - academically and morally.

Daddy had a heart attack, and his rantings begin to grow faint. With the realization that he wouldn't be around forever, mine did too. I was bound and determined to make his last days more peaceful. But women started enlisting in the service, and he worried that one of us might have to go to war. I reminded him that, although we were brave enough to carry on his patriotic spirit, we were all three too old to enlist. But he insisted that the next fight would be right here in our own back yard.

"I smell the smoke of oppression hanging all over our country" he whispered, with tears streaming down his face, "but I lack the strength and social skills to put out the fire, and heaven knows there's precious little time left. You'd better write my congressman," he ordered.

"And Daddy, just who would that be?" I asked teasingly, when Mom wasn't around to keep me from ruffling his feathers. I doubted he even knew who his congressman was, and I was sure he'd never written to him. But Dad insisted that I do as he said, not as he did. And for once, I chose not to argue. He was hurting so, and I ached to ease his pain, so I held his rough and calloused hand, and listened. But before he finished dictating that letter, he drifted off to sleep - leaving me to grope for the right words to say.

Fallout From A Fake Utopia

Zealous to satisfy my daddy's cry for freedom, I got into chasing the American dream - for everybody. Although I contributed little, my generation accomplished a lot: we put man on the moon, and embarked on programs to save the environment; we cured diseases, transplanted organs, and expanded everyone's life cycle by at least two decades; we reached new depths in human understanding; we did our best to make war a battle between machines, not men; we built financial empires; we provided our kids the opportunity to go to college, and the chance to become millionaires in greater numbers than ever before; we made them a super power among the nations, and prepared them to embrace the universe; we advanced technology so rapidly that even we couldn't keep up with it.

But while we were busy making all that progress, the government grew, and the decent society we took for granted fell by the wayside. I guess we made one big mistake - in a democracy, ruled for and of and by the people, we failed to govern ourselves, our leaders, and consequently our nation.

Yes, we were striving to advance all the right causes: freedom, equality, environmental preservation, justice, and the opportunity for every member of our society to excel. But we entrusted government to do the supervising for us. And as governments have done throughout history, ours gladly accommodated - to our detriment of course. From city and township, to county, to state, to regional zoning offices, all the way up to the feds - at least five levels of government came swarming in to lead the parade. Each level gave birth to regulatory departments and commissions and divisions and boards and agencies, faster than we could type out their names.

Not just at the national level, but everywhere we lived, bureaucrats started passing more repetitive ambiguous regulations than we could even read, let alone understand and live by. And as we sifted through the murky rhetoric for truths and solutions we could not find, they took our rights away faster than we could switch through the channels on our television sets. Was it a giant conspiracy to overtake us? No - it was just a few little politicians with greedy private agendas.

Certainly we needed change for the better. But as always, government was the wrong entity to entrust with the duty to improve. Leaders recognized every good cause we came up with as an opportunity to make themselves rich and famous. And the more we willingly paid, the deeper they buried us in confusion and fear. Their subtle propaganda pitted black against white, women against men, rich against poor, good against bad, sick against well, and young against old. They even pitted us against our children and Mother Nature.

Before we knew it, we had more problems getting along together, and more reason to buy government intervention than ever before. But no matter how much we conceded, or how much the disadvantaged supposedly gained - our social dilemmas did not diminish. While we were exchanging one set of oppressions for another, only the government got bigger and stronger, while the elements of decency and freedom slipped farther and farther away from our grasp. But - lest we might err - we let leaders continue to use our causes and concerns to lure us further and further into their greedy maze.

For fear we might tread on the rights of others, we forfeited our own. We conceded our right to defend ourselves and our property, for fear we would treat bad guys unjustly. Yet giving criminals more leeway did not protect our society from crime - the fairer our judgement, the higher the crime rate soared. And at this very moment, for fear we are drug smugglers and terrorists, Congress debates taking our rights to privacy away.

For fear we might cheat and take advantage of each other, we forfeited the right to operate our businesses freely, and government bureaucracies prospered at our expense. For fear we could not take care of our needy, we forfeited the right to keep most of our profits. Yet the more trillions we paid, the more hungry and homeless and helpless we saw. Poverty increased at an alarming rate, right along with bureaucratic waste.

When we questioned their social programs, they forced us to give jobs to the elderly and raised the minimum wage. But that did not ease the burdens of those too old to work, or take the load of big government off the backs of those too poor to invest in the future. When we asked for better special-care facilities, they demanded we forfeit the right to shelter our handicapped, and forced us to mingle with the contagiously ill. But that did not enable the weak and lame to rise up and walk - it furthered the spread of disease.

For fear we could not treat each other equally, we settled for reverse discrimination, instead of true equality for all. But quotas did not end our racial strife, enable our disadvantaged, nor mend our failing relationships.

We relinquished our right to discipline our children, for fear we would abuse them. We abandoned our moral code, for fear it was too old fashioned. We forfeited our right to pray in public, and gave the NEA control of our schools. But none of that educated our children or prevented violence within their ranks, and it certainly didn't earn us their respect.

For fear we would someday destroy the earth, we learned to support the present generation while preserving enough environmental resources to sustain those to come. But the government still bought up our land, granted our private property rights to animals and weeds, and contaminated our waters with nuclear testing.

And isn't it a shame - we who tamed the Wild West can't even traipse through our national parks without a government chaperon; we who cleaned up the environment can't recycle our trash without government supervision; and we who built skyscrapers can't fix our roofs without a government permit. Kids who bungi jump and skateboard over cement walls can't even ride bicycles on the sidewalk without a helmet. The people who put a man on the moon must now stay off the streets when the government says they're too slippery. If our fathers were alive today, they'd say the government has us right where it wants us - too confused and too scared to be free. And they'd be right.

The government's fake attempts to regulate us into Utopia have complicated our society and overwhelmed our individual common sense so far into apathetic submission that everything an ordinary person should and could do to preserve democracy in a decent society seems frightfully impossible.

Politics are so intimidating and expensive that ordinary people refuse to run for elective office. Because we can't be trusted to oust a leader when it's time, term limitations have been placed upon our elected representatives. And it's so hard to tell the good guys from the bad that too many of us don't even bother voting anymore.

Our laws have become so ambiguous and unenforceable that we're afraid to seek justice. It's harder on the victim than on the criminal, and so expensive that the innocent just can't afford to pick up the tab. Jury duty has become so difficult that most ordinary citizens resort to thinking up answers that will get them dismissed, while others disclose secret court antics for financial gain. Juror selection, and the process of presenting evidence has become a quagmire of legal maneuvers - so bad that the government has us almost talked into giving up the jury system and the right to be judged by our peers. But the criminals are still running free.

The latest history books give our freedom fighters an oppressive brutal slant. And as the government presses the younger generation into law and order, "brutal" is what our kids think freedom is all about. The world is losing track of Americans who died for liberty and justice, and those of us who are old enough to know better won't speak out - for fear of being labeled "politically incorrect."

Today we're on a merry-go-round, pressed and bound for a utopia we'll never reach. The government has no intention of slowing down to let us off, and at this rate of speed, we're afraid to jump. So we just keep giving in, and going 'round with whichever politician happens to be riding the shiniest horse.

But in our hearts and minds we know better. The more billions we are forced to pay, the wealthier and more powerful Uncle Sam gets, and the less peace and prosperity we see. Our heads nod in fearful assent, while our common sense screams its warning - "This is not for your our own good." But the more questions we ask, the more confusing and frightening the propaganda becomes. You're hearing all those mixed musical messages, aren't you?

They say the crime rate is down two per cent, but the nightly news is one criminal horror story after another, followed by more advertisements for security alarms. Neighborhood watch patrols are being deputized by the hundreds, and the President says we need double the police force. They say our schools must be gated to keep criminals out, but fifty-three percent of offenders are kids, and our children are shooting each other in the hallways.

They tell us the Cold War is over, yet China and India are still testing bombs, and Russia still sells arms to our enemies. Terrorist threats send chills down our spines. Rumors of chemical warfare, oil embargoes, scattered battle cries, and secret attacks still cost us billions, and still threaten the lives of our youths.

They say we're the strongest people on earth, but the government has to take care of us. Right now we're being spared from too much land use, the bad business practices of our free enterprise system, over-exposure to religion, bad weather and natural disasters, accidental injury, and our own human errors. They've banned us from slippery streets, put helmets on our kids, and evicted us from our wilderness trails - all for our own good. As we gasp for a breath of free air, they eliminate smoking guns, and declare fifty-seven percent of us in need of some degree of rehabilitation. What will they be saving us from next - ourselves, overcrowding on our highways and byways, oversized sports utility vehicles, mad cow disease, and global warming?

The government is growing at a phenomenal rate. While we stand quietly by waiting for asteroids from space to fall on our heads, government leaders make our choices and decisions for us. And as we beg them to control every aspect of our lives, and pay them to fix every dilemma, they laugh all the way to the bank. Wouldn't it be funny if, after all the battles we've fought and won for freedom, we accidently slipped, and fell into socialism? HELLO.

Good morning, Silent Majority. We have been sleeping too long, and it's time to wake up. Our forefathers left us a government for and of and by the people, and a peaceful process by which to preserve life, liberty, and the pursuit of happiness. It's called "majority rule." And we, the strong and capable, decent, sensible citizens of this country are still the majority. We not only have the power to shed this government-inflicted utopian oppression, we have a responsibility to restore and preserve freedom.

As our leaders advocate taking more of our freedoms for the good of all, passing more laws for our protection, and launching more social programs that appear to eradicate the classes, just remember - history clearly shows that, in the process of creating a perfect socialistic society, only the government gets big and rich. And all the ordinary people become equally oppressed.

Remember - as the rights of the majority go, so go the rights of everybody else in the country. When the majority looses their individual freedoms, nobody is free. When the rights of criminals take priority over law abiding citizens, nobody is safe. When the majority loses their private property rights, nobody owns land. When the press is silenced by government, nobody learns the truth. When taxes and administrative costs bankrupt the majority, the whole nation lives in poverty and oppression. When the majority of our children come under government's latchkey, all our youthful free spirits die.

We must rely on ourselves as much as humanly possible, for when the government starts taking care of the majority of us, the nation will be neither healthy, nor free. We know democratic free enterprise will never be utopia, and that a few less capable may suffer as we prosper. But under government control all the people are incapable and everybody suffers -except the few in charge at the top. Just imagine beautiful tress, clear running streams, spacious blue skies, purple mountain majesties, and amber waves of grain - in an America where no one is free.

All through history, governments have gone to great lengths to gain control of their people. But once control is theirs, no government in history has ever voluntarily relinquished it back to the people without a fight - at great sacrifice to and of the masses. Our government is already too powerful to defeat with military machines. If we don't preserve freedom now, while we still have the right to vote and protest peacefully, the next generation will never know liberty. We must restore freedom now. It's the dawn of a new day, and we who have kept quiet too long must start calling the shots.

RACISM BE GONE

In my line of work, I must complete many government forms which require a check mark by my race. My grandmother said I was half English and Dutch, part Irish, and one-eighth Cherokee Indian. But the way my ancestors screwed around, who knows. One thing's for sure though - I am a U.S citizen. But wouldn't you know it - there's no such designation on most government forms. When I express doubt as to how to answer their racial questions correctly, the government agent sitting across from me shrugs as she looks at my physical characteristics and then says "Just check Caucasian." Did somebody say "divided we fall?"

My Daddy always said government was to blame for our racial tensions. And his most memorable lecture on the subject went something like:

> "For centuries our leaders have been putting us into red, yellow, black, and white categories. By pointing out our differences, and appealing to our sense of racial pride, they've fed our fears and stirred our hatreds - just enough to keep us divided. They've pitted us against each other, and given the orders for war. As we wallowed in the stench of death upon their battle fields, they bathed in fame and glory. As we fought each other in the turmoil they created, and toiled in poverty through the aftermath of war, they relished in the bounties we captured. They drained our united strength just enough- just enough to keep us producing their power and wealth."

Recently, I heard both President Clinton and Jesse Jackson say that instead of living in the past, we should put it behind us. I know we can't always believe everything they say, but this time they made some sense, with one slight exception - if we are to keep Daddy's history from repeating itself, we must learn from its mistakes, and never ever forget its lessons.

It's hard to examine our diverse histories from a fair and objective perspective, let alone learn from them. Depending on who's doing the teaching, we hear a different version of the truth: European forefathers were oppressive capitalists; Africans were cannibals; the Spanish were pirates; Asians were imperial murderers; Indians were scalping savages; and all were barbaric tyrants and war mongers. With each lecture, the ordinary people of every race only seem to learn one thing - to be more and more prejudiced against each other.

We've been indoctrinated to believe that we had to fight each other to feed and protect our families, maintain our identity, worship our own God, and pursue freedom and prosperity. Consequently all of us have endured hardship, and committed sins against each other at the hands of manipulative powerful leaders. And to hear them tell it, none of us are any good.

But we must never forget that when racial oppression runs rampant, only the authoritarians who perpetuate the conflict are protected from slaughter. And only the victorious leaders reap the rewards after a conquest. The suffering and death of the masses is never limited by color. And the bounties are never harvested by the ordinary people of any race.

Many of our grandparents died in Indian and civil wars-all because a few leaders didn't want liberty and justice for all. We even had to amend our own Constitution in order to emancipate slaves and women. And think about World War II - by the time it was over, millions of people who didn't even know why they hated, had killed each other off. And millions more were left living in fear and poverty. Europe, Japan, North Africa, and the South Pacific lay in ruins. As ordinary people anguished, leaders bathed in luxury and held great summit talks. They signed treaties that left an Israeli nation in conflict, Germans divided by the Berlin Wall, a vast Communist block, the ordinary people of this planet with the threat of nuclear extinction, and enough fear and prejudice to start another war. In the aftermath, we praised and empowered the winners as they promised to rebuild our devastated lands - and all because one little man pitted one race against another.

Of course we vowed never to allow anyone to provoke us into destroying the homes and lives of that many people ever again. But since then we've killed each other off by the tens of thousands in places like Korea, Vietnam, South America, Bosnia, Iraq, and right here on the streets of America. At this very moment our leaders are signing treaties and gathering riches, while ordinary people in war-ravaged countries struggle to overcome starvation and pain. And while some Americans weep at the monuments of their battle-scarred dead, others are still fighting each other right out in the streets.

Given our many years of diverse backgrounds and indoctrinations, it is difficult to admit our similarities, and to respect each other's right to be different. But then we've been programmed to blame and fear and take advantage of each other for centuries - and old habits die hard. Naturally, old prejudices still seep into our hearts and minds. But we can overcome.

It's time we admitted that we have just enough similarities to end the political manipulation that has victimized us for centuries. There is no such thing as red, or yellow, or black, or white people. In reality we are all some shade of brown - from the palest flesh tone to the darkest tan. And we all have red blood. We also have the same basic human needs to feed, protect, and educate our children, to be safe in our homes and on our streets, to excel and prosper, to live in peace, and to freely pursue happiness. And in America, we all still have the same basic Constitutional rights to do so.

Granted some of us were born here, some of us voluntarily traveled here, and some of us were forced here. But no matter how beautiful our homelands were, how great our cultures may have been, or how unjust our conquerings and uprootings were, the fact is that no country on earth has remained the same over the years. And none of our peoples can undo or return to the past.

No matter how we got here, where we came from, or why we came, we are in the United States of America as it is today. Even though we still face serious social dilemmas and an overbearing government, being here is not so bad. Nowhere else on earth have so many ordinary people, from so many different nationalities, overcome so many adversities, survived such great oppressions, fought and died side by side for freedom, and blended such a variety of beautiful cultures. Never have so many ordinary people from so many different places come together and prospered as one nation so successfully. And never have so many extraordinary people from so many different backgrounds worked together as peace keepers and humanitarians to share that prosperity with the world - even shared with civilizations thousands of years older than our own.

Today we are free and equal. The majority of us are finally working, shopping, playing, and learning together. We are entertaining each other and admiring each other's heroes. We are even eating and worshiping together. And just as the good and ordinary people of every race and creed have joined to make it so, the good and ordinary people of every race and creed must join to keep it so - for it is evident that, although those in power today are a little more subtle about it, they are still propagating racial tension, and profiting from its embrace.

In a free society wherein all men are created equal, when we can't kid around about our dining preferences without creating news of racial strife, somebody out there is deliberately trying to heat us up to the boiling point. And it's not Tiger Woods or the ex-Kmart employee who got fired for suggesting they get together for some ethnic food. I couldn't understand why suggesting chicken and collard greens was considered a racial slur, but according to the media it was. When my old hillbilly Grandma was alive she served fried chicken and collard greens every Sunday, and she never threw a slur at anyone except

Grandpa. We were all mighty proud to sit down at her table. Too bad the rest of the world isn't as naive as I am - we'd have a lot less to get insulted about.

Understandably, the power structure is worried - and no wonder. If this trend of togetherness continues, racism could disappear, along with too many of their reasons to collect trillions of our tax dollars. Naturally, leaders would prefer that we stay too preoccupied with racial differences to notice things like police brutality and government waste.

But if we are to remain a racially peaceful and free nation, we must forgive past sins and avoid past mistakes, allow for each other's differences, trust our accomplishments and similarities, bring the few stragglers up to date, and cure our social ills by expanding on the positive foundation we have. We must start passing the bread to each other, instead of to the gluttonous government that stands between us. Ordinary Americans of every race and creed must unite, to be free.

Ebonics - Another Language Barrier

Some years back, headlines pitted poverty in underprivileged black ghettoes against affluent white suburbs. Minorities believed we thought they were subhuman, and we were so afraid of them that we probably did. Scandalous reports portrayed blacks as underprivileged terrorists, ripping the clothes from oppressive white backs. And all it did was make ordinary Americans of both colors more and more scared of each other.

Martin Luther King and John F. Kennedy seemed to have understood and began moving us toward some feelings of equality. But somebody shot them down in the street. We will never know for sure who had them killed, or why. We only know that succeeding leaders from both sides put us back at each others' throats.

Lyndon Johnson and Jesse Jackson moved in to bring their own kind of peace -the kind that left money and power in their hands. Remember the day they sat down for talks? They were chauffeured to the White House door in limousines, surrounded by bodyguards, and all dressed up in the best suits money could buy. In that elegant conference room, from shiny crystal and silver, they were served all that rich food. They wiped their chins on linen napkins, and patted themselves on the back for easing our tensions. With soothing voices, white leaders took credit for mending past injustices, and black leaders boasted that they had overcome. But ordinary Americans of every color paid for the progress with more taxes and regulations than ever before. We went back to work like puppets on a string - leaving our pay checks and our businesses in the firm grip of the Feds.

Like many in the country's heartland, my family remained poor. We used an outhouse in the dead of winter. Mom carried water from the well and buckets of coal to the pot-bellied stove where she heated it. She filled the wash tub with hot water, while Grandma held sheets against the wall of the old house we rented, to keep snow from blowing in through the cracks while we bathed. And Daddy worked longer hours to pay his share of the extra taxes.

While leaders pretended to pump billions of dollars into upgrading housing and schools, poverty and violence in the ghetto worsened. Pictures on the nightly news depicted blacks destroying the very neighborhoods we'd sacrificed so much to build. Both races kicked and screamed, and called each other names. And as ordinary Americans of every color swirled in anger, fear, and confusion, the government, who'd torn us apart in the first place, sent in troops to force us back together again.

George Wallace and Malcolm X led a parade of destruction that violated the highest law of the land - The Constitution of the United States of America. But instead of arresting them, federal leaders sent in troops to put ordinary citizens back in line, and then passed more laws they didn't intend to enforce against themselves.

On television we watched little kids from Cleveland's inner city standing in the cold blowing snow at 6:00 a.m. without boots and coats, waiting for busses that would take them to a school miles away from home. After dark they arrived back at their bus stops, tramped through danger zones, and arrived home - too cold, hungry, and tired to study. Their mothers, most of whom couldn't afford transportation, were excluded from participating in their education. The news said most were black, but I saw a lot of Spanish, Asian, and Caucasian kids there.

In turn, middle-class children were bussed from the suburbs to schools in the inner city. They too left home early, facing deteriorated conditions and dangers they never before knew existed. They too arrived home late, uncomfortable, disillusioned, scared, hungry, and too tired to study. The news said most of them were white, but there were a mixture of races there too.

Daddy raved on about leaders (black and white alike), bridging their way to more personal wealth and control by deliberately clouding the issue of integration with that of getting a quality education. He'd say things like "If they'd teach the right stuff, segregation would disappear on its own," and "Bussing will cost more than new schools and good books, but it won't teach our kids as much." He ranted about the dangers of government-forced schooling too far away from home. He figured little kids of every race needed to stay close to their mothers, and that the richest country in the world could afford to provide every one of them an education near home - no matter what color they were, or where they lived. But his words just added to the turmoil, and were soon drowned out by more accusations of racism.

The National Education Association took charge of our local schools. And with NEA running the show, the interaction between children and their parents, both at home and at school, was seriously impaired by legal and economic restraints. Less affluent families were separated in the name of racial equality. Middle class mothers dropped their kids off, and went on to work to help their families keep up with new taxes. Gasoline prices soared. And once again, already rich and powerful black and white politicians got another pay raise, more recognition, and more votes.

Under more powerful leadership, armed guards, and an even heavier tax load, the ordinary people of every race conceded to equal opportunity education through mandatory bussing; and our children learned to live with its hardships. But poverty and ignorance continued to increase without racial boundaries, both in the ghetto and throughout the countryside. And American children of every color got left out in the cold academically. Their moral and academic status has been slipping down-hill ever since.

And now, just as we're finally working and playing together, and finally starting to demand less government control and real educational improvements for all our children in unison - "Ebonics" pops up to create division among us over dialect. Remember the Bible's Tower of Babel? Divided by a language barrier, the people fell.

Jesse Jackson insults his own people by saying "African-American adults can't communicate with their children, and then he pulls whites into the struggle by blaming "their" schools for teaching the wrong things. Somebody needs to bring him up to speed. Dark brown citizens are not Africans, and there are no such things as white schools. Jackson demands big business pay millions of dollars to minority kids for damage supposedly caused by lack of opportunity. But you see how he spends the money - traveling around in five-star luxury, to promote a new and separate language that does not exist. I guess he's still practicing for the Presidency.

And Bill Clinton insults all races, by waffling to attract the vote of whichever color crowd he's in front of - assuring every one of us that the NEA will investigate the language problem and get a firm grip on the matter. He's looking more like Lyndon Johnson every day.

There is no denying that we need some changes in education. But giving government the control was not the answer thirty years ago, it isn't the answer today, and it never will be. As we watch NEA officials destroy the quality of education, and witness the soaring crime rate among school children, the thought of giving NEA more control makes us all frightened for our kids. There has got to be a better way.

In searching my life's experiences for possible alternatives, I reminisced about the back-woods of southern Ohio and West Virginia, where I was raised. As the first granddaughter, I enjoyed many precious moments chatting with Grandma. She had a hillbilly accent that wouldn't quit. And although none of the family before me had much formal education, they were pretty smart. Grandma was self taught and a great communicator. She explained the bad and the good about the primitive wild West, about the Indians I descended from, and about my ancestors from across the sea. I learned to overcome the evils and to appreciate the beauty of my roots. And I'm proud of my history in a special way that no stranger could be expected to understand.

But my grandmother wanted more for me than the tents and tribes, religious wars, and rulings by kings that I'd descended from. So she insisted that I replace that Hillbilly accent with the English in my text book. And when I passed the beauty and pride of that heritage on to my three children, I too insisted that they reach out for more. Today one is a youth minister, one teaches handicapped children, and one is a business manager. If Grandma were still alive, she'd be proud of the first college-educated generation in our family. And she'd want all Americans to be equally as free.

No matter what dialect we used, my family never needed anybody's help to communicate love and respect to each other, nor to teach each other right from wrong. And neither do the families in America today. If a few are lacking, the rest of us can reach out to help. We'll do better by our kids if we help them build on the foundation language we already have, than we will by letting the government charge us for a new one.

Historically, all our forefathers communicated in several different tongues, and even those who spoke the same language broke it up into a variety of dialects. But no matter who made the choice years ago, or which accents and slang words we've added to distinguish our different regions of the globe, Americans have been left with standard English as their most prominent foundation language. Our Constitution is written in it, as are our text books, our laws, our directions, and our street signs. It is the only sure mode of communication for the vast majority of our citizens here at home. And because it has become the universal language of business and prosperity everywhere, foreign countries are demanding that their children learn it too.

Both President Clinton and Jesse Jackson speak it "loud and clear" when they push for a global economy. Yet both leaders show their true anti-American colors when they refuse to designate it as our official tongue. Their explanations get a little muddled when we ask why American kids of every race are slipping academically. Both get even harder to understand when we ask what happens to all that money we pay for quality in education. And both Jackson and Clinton become down-right deaf, dumb, and mute when we ask how much a new language will cost, or who'll really benefit from the bill.

But Americans know. New languages won't help reduce crime and poverty, nor educate our children any more than bussing did. What they will do is divert funds from an already-struggling educational system and deny more American kids the opportunity to learn. They will provide the government another excuse to collect more taxes, and further separate our peoples. They will promote a personal agenda for current black and white leaders, at the expense of ordinary Americans everywhere. And they will cause our kids to fall farther behind the rest of the world - and that translates into "a more disadvantaged America."

My daddy used to say, "Children aren't born prejudiced; they're taught to fear and hate." Isn't it time we taught our kids to hate oppressive government, instead of each other?

As we move toward a global economy, let's pool our resources to provide all the nation's children an education that will enable them to achieve and excel individually, both at home and abroad. Let's spare them the racial strife of another language barrier, by demanding that the educational system we support teach them to read, write, and speak our foundation language fluently.

Perhaps, as fluent communicators of the same tongue, they will do a better job of understanding each other than we have done. And as they come together as one people, of the same language, perhaps they'll demand better results from their social programs, better performance from their servants in government, and the best for themselves, their America, and all its citizens.

MORE REVERSE DISCRIMINATION

Admittedly, one time when I saw President Clinton attending so many different worship services on Easter Sunday, I wrenched in disrespect. It's not that I'm prejudiced against any of those churches he went to. I just find it disturbing that the man who freely worships with so many different gods heads up the government that stifles my right to pray to one. I figured it indicated that he valued getting votes more than he valued standing up for the principles of his true belief. Then somebody reminded me that he doesn't have any principles. But I'm still not inclined to deny him religious freedom - just my vote.

And as if having a dictatorial President without principles isn't bad enough, the Christian Coalition started another movement to amend the Constitution. They want a new amendment guaranteeing us the right to pray in school. Don't get me wrong. I'm all for prayer in school. But we already have that constitutional right.

When I began ranting that "Instead of changing it, they should be defending and supporting the Constitution we already have," my sister disagreed. Barb still prefers playing house to getting politically involved. But now that she's a little older, I get an occasional response from her - always opposite mine of course. She feels that exercising one's right to religious freedom in public might not be fair to those who do not share the same beliefs. And she even suggested that I might be biased against other faiths.

Me prejudiced? I don't think so. I'd never deprive another of his or her rights. Sure my mother thought that to be anything but a Christian-Protestant-Nazarene was heathen. But she also taught us that even our God gave people a choice. Over the years, my friends have been everything from Atheists to Hindus, and I certainly never felt like denying any of them their religious preferences. When my teenage children wanted to become Baptists, I applauded their choosing. And when my daughter up and married a Catholic, all I did was thank God for a son-in-law willing to teach me the new bedtime prayers by which we tuck in my grandchildren.

A friend of mine, who happens to be an Atheist, agrees with me, and assures me that he and I are the least prejudiced people he knows. "You attend the Nazarene Church, but you don't expect anyone else to accommodate you by forfeiting their constitutional right to choose otherwise. And I prefer to date single blond women, but the fact that you are a married brunette does not keep me from respecting you as a human being," he teased.

When I interjected a prayer for his lost soul into the blessing over lunch, he snickered, and read the newspaper. "Constitutional freedom of religion doesn't force me, or anyone else, to participate when you pray," he said; "It just gives us all the right to if we so choose, and I don't choose to. Besides, replacing your right to pray, with my right not to is reverse discrimination. And that takes freedom away from everybody - including me. So for the sake of freedom, I tolerate your prayers."

"How noble", I smirked. And we went on to discuss reverse discrimination in more detail. We considered the possibility that our vantage points might make it too easy for us to brush off the historical injustices and hardships that prejudicial beliefs have caused so many people. So I decided to do a little more soul searching - sorting out all the beliefs I'd picked up along my life's journey, to see if I was biased toward others in different ways.

In spite of chaotic leadership and hateful propaganda, I'd resolved the racial issue in my heart. Fortunately, I'd been taught to judge people by their individual actions, not by the shade of brown upon their skin. And since religious instruction had been the most rigorous part of my upbringing, it seemed to be the place to start my checkup.

I went back to Barb - the sister who didn't think the Constitution gave Christians the right to pray in public. She posed an interesting question: "Since the Constitution gives Atheists rights too, when there's a clash, whose rights are more important?" Of course, the way I see things, allowing everyone a choice is freedom. And forcing either side to concede is oppression. So before we knew it, we were caught up in that age-old debate over what the Constitution really says, and how fair it really is to anybody.

Again, my Atheist friend assured me that my opinion was founded on constitutional principle, but he couldn't remember the exact verbiage. In fact, nobody I talked with knew exactly what the Constitution really said. And neither did I. Most of us had gone to school and had run around the country proclaiming certain truths to be our inalienable Constitutional rights, because that's what we'd been told. But sadly, none of us had ever read the document that made our country the first nation in history to be founded on individual liberties. So I headed straight for the library and got a copy.

The first ten amendments is "The Bill of Rights." And the first amendment under that Bill of Rights says, "Congress shall make no law respecting an establishment of religion, or prohibiting the free exercise thereof; or abridging the freedom of speech, or of the press; or the right of the people peaceably to assemble." Notice that the Constitution guarantees us freedom "of" religion, "of" speech, "of" press, and "of" assembly; and it never mentions the word "from".

The dictionary defines "of" as "belonging to." The word "from," as defined by that same dictionary, means "denied, separated, away, and apart from." The fact is, our Constitution guarantees us freedom "of" everything, including religion; not freedom "from" anything except government oppression. And it does not say "so long as we keep those freedoms in the closet, or just at home, or only in church, or out of school." It neither limits the number of participants who can assemble for the purpose of practicing religion freely, nor forces any quotas upon us. And it does not say "so long as we keep the exercise thereof separated from those who disagree or prefer otherwise."

Being forced to give up my religious freedom to those with a different concept caused a resentful feeling to creep into my soul. But it never occurred to me to blame the government. Instead, I'd been directing my anger toward the demanding faces of all those anti-Christian demonstrators I saw - until today, when I read the Constitution. The Constitution does not protect us from each other's choices. In fact, the Constitution does not regulate us at all - it regulates government and prohibits government from interfering with our lives. We should all send copies to our representatives. They obviously haven't read it either.

My Atheist friend pointed out that leaders exploit the masses by manipulating the Constitution, and that by allowing them to do so, we all play right into the government's hand. "They don't want me to laugh at your ridiculous prayers; they want me to pay and praise them for making you stop," he said. He went on to lecture, something like this - "Leaders are the shepherds of conflict, gathering money and power from the ordinary people who are willing to follow them. Whether they be heads of state, preachers in charge of churches, or chieftains of a minority group, leaders must have a cause - a purpose for which to solicit the funds and support that provide and justify their living. So they find a group with an axe to grind; and if they can't find a gripe, they stir one up. The more conflicts we have, the more money and power it takes for them to resolve things for us."

This friend reminded me too much of Daddy. But the truth in what he said made me feel justified in my beliefs, and inspired me to direct my anger away from my fellow citizens, toward the real culprits - government leaders inciting riots just to get money and power.

As I went on to explore other areas of possible bias, several friends and relatives anxiously jumped on my diagnostic bandwagon. My sisters couldn't wait to get into a discussion about gender discrimination. While I was struggling with my third husband, they were both celebrating twenty-five year marriages to the same husbands, and still counting. And they were sure I was prejudiced against men.

Admittedly, Caucasian men had been the most powerful ruling force I'd had to overcome. Only because I forced the issue did my father give me more leeway than he gave most girls. And if he'd had a son with which to share his throne, I'm not so sure he would have. Even so, it took a lot of stubborn resolve for me to overcome the limitations Dad placed on females. Male chauvinism was in the air everywhere when I was growing up. Even my religion placed men at the head of the household. And although I refused to walk openly in that light, I blamed its subtle effect on my subconscious mind for the fact that I got pregnant and married instead of staying in school - maybe just a convenient excuse for avoiding accepting responsibility for my own mistaken choices.

Anyway, my battle for freedom raged on through two failed marriages - the second of which got violent at times. I recall thinking my husband was a sadistic brute every time he struck me, while feeling totally justified when I slugged him. Barb was quick to point out just how prejudiced and illegal that double standard was. "In a free county, what's fair for the goose is fair for the gander," she said, "and anything else is reverse discrimination. We all have the right to be safe, and we each have a responsibility to act decently."

"Too bad our law makers and enforcement officers didn't realize that the right to safety and decency was not limited by gender, age, race, or any of the other categories they put us into. If they had, we'd all have been given equal protection under one law, instead of all those ambiguous regulations and agencies set up to deal with specifics like domestic and racial violence," I muttered.

"There you go again," my sister said, "unfairly labeling the whole male segment of society because of the actions of a few leaders and lawmen." She reminded me that we'd never have gotten the Emancipation Proclamation or Women's Suffrage without all the ordinary men who willingly fought and died for our freedom, right alongside us. Of course she was right. And I had to admit that in our democracy, even Caucasian men had to be given equality.

By the time I got this far into my self-evaluation, I was feeling pretty confident that any prejudices I had developed over the years were overcome. And then entered my only daughter, Susan (the one who teaches handicapped children), insisting that I was prejudiced against the handicapped and elderly. She was quick to point out that I'd been blessed to have three healthy children, and that although I wasn't old enough to be senile, I was getting there fast.

Susan suggested that I start thinking with my heart instead of my head. And I was trying to do that when our local Winn-Dixie started hiring the elderly and the handicapped. But I just couldn't resist complaining. The government set quotas, and subsidized the payment of their wages. The store used our tax dollars to pay their help. But instead of seeing the savings reflected on my register receipt, prices went up. And on top of that, I was expected to tip a carryout who was less capable of toting my groceries than I was.

I know they say the goal is to help everyone live life as richly as possible. And while that old man, trying to carry and load groceries in Florida's summer heat, may have been making Winn-Dixie and the government richer, the only thing he looked like he was about to get was a stroke. So I took Susan's advice, and went with my heart instead of my head. My head said "Don't perpetuate this farce." But I let the old man walk beside me, while I carried my own groceries. And I tipped him anyway.

I shot off my mouth to a nearby nurse - "It's a shame that in a country as rich as ours, that old man's social security can't afford him retirement." But when the nurse informed me that he could well afford anything he wanted, and just needed something to do, I got mad. I'm not sure whether he suckered me in, or whether the government and Winn-Dixie did. But either way, none of them will get the chance to again. I'll shop someplace else.

Never are the dilemmas of a free society more manifest than when we stand face to face with a handicapped child or help an elderly person across the street. Our hearts go out to them. And in the depths of our souls, we identify with them - for we were once all helpless babes, and we shall all grow old and faint someday. But present affirmative action policies are both a disservice to those disadvantaged, and an injustice to the rest of society.

We are of a scientific mind. And no matter how harsh the realities, we know that the ill, the lame, and the weak cannot support our species - not even if we are one of them. We know that a society cannot survive by promoting its least capable at the expense of the fittest. And we know we must find a better way to care for and entertain these needy - a way that does not perpetuate the government while draining the strength and resources of its strongest citizens.

I know my attitude is considered "insensitive" by those who advocate mainstreaming the profound and severely handicapped, and the disease ridden. But just the opposite is true. No matter the physical size, the minds and spirits of the human infantile and the sick call out for more nurturing - not the kind of pressure necessary to propel mainstream society successfully onto a higher level, in a competitive and complicated world. And no one will ever be able to convince me that putting our weak, sick, elderly and disabled to work will ever be the best thing for anybody, except the government and big businesses who profit from their infirm conditions.

They need care, not pressure to compete and keep up. Think about how you feel when you have a common cold. Of course you wish it weren't so. But that doesn't take the misery out of going to work, or trying to keep up with the swim team. Think how you feel, when you're a little overweight and can't lose those extra pounds, or when you're running behind everybody else in the race. Do you want somebody constantly pushing you to do better, or do you long to be among friends who accept you the way you are? How 'bout some real compassion here?

It's time we pushed aside the aspirations of those who wish to profit from these causes and took better care of ourselves and our disadvantaged. It's time we stopped these false indoctrinations. To the tune of millions of dollars (most of which government puts in its pocket), handicapped children are afforded every educational advantage in public schools, while mainstream children attending the same schools do without. Many of these disadvantaged kids are too retarded to even learn to feed and toilet themselves, let alone ever comprehend reading or writing. And many of them are HIV positive.

Case in point: A pitiful county somewhere in North Carolina is pretty typical of most public schools across our country. Regular classrooms are over-crowded and lacking educational tools - thirty-plus students to one teacher, and not enough money for updated text books. But special classes, with only seven profoundly physically and mentally handicapped students per class, have several assistants in addition to a special education teacher. Most of these students cannot feed or toilet themselves, and are incapable of ever learning to do so. Others are so seriously impaired that they will never even be able to function at the kindergarten level, let alone ever be productive members of society. All can remain in class until age twenty-one, although they are exceptionally strong, and sometimes violent. Because they cannot comprehend the difference between positive and negative behavior, their teachers must be state certified in restraint tactics - special techniques necessary to physically prevent them from harming themselves and others in the classroom. One particular student comes to mind - an HIV positive twenty year old who has a tendency to bite others, especially when she has to do anything against her will. She has the mind of a two-year-old; and the size, strength, and will of a 175-pound adult male. A teacher, who was bitten while trying to prevent this student from injuring another, has to be tested for AIDS periodically for the rest of her life - or until the virus shows up.

I know they say the AIDS virus is only transmitted sexually or by blood. Well, biting and other physical jousting between school children draws blood. Besides, common sense tells us that if AIDS can be transferred from one person to another by two bodily fluids, there's a good possibility that it can be transmitted by others - probably even saliva and snotty noses. But just as we didn't know thalidomide caused deformed babies, or that blacks with syphilis were being used for experimental purposes, or that nuclear testing would pollute our environment, we may never know how contagious the AIDS virus is until it's too late for our children.

Those of us who know enough to quarantine our kids when they get chicken pox must use our heads accordingly on other health issues. Having to work and go to school with those infected with AIDS, and being forced to rub shoulders with those who perpetuate the spread of this deadly disease is a disaster for the species. They call that "chemical warfare" when Saddam Hussein does it, not affirmative action. And they put the lives of our boys on the line, trying to kill it off over there. For the sake of our children, don't you think it's time we ended it over here?

It's hard to believe that the government spends millions of tax dollars, and passes thousands of regulations, to squelch individual liberties for the sake of a healthy society, and then turns right around and expends more to force healthy Americans into contact with a disease as deadly as AIDS. If that don't wake us up to the fact that America is being exposed to the world's oldest, most dangerous epidemic (government oppression), nothing will.

Society survives and functions because most of its members are physically and mentally fit. And human compassion drives us to take better care of our weak and lame than most species do; which is as it should be. But, whether it be the automobile, the environment, or the human mind, body, and spirit - we must protect and maintain the vehicle that keeps us going, and gets us where we have to be. Neither the species nor its free society will survive if we do otherwise. And we must rely on ourselves as much as humanly possible, for when the government starts taking care of the majority of us, the nation will be neither healthy, nor free.

With that in mind, no matter how hard I tried, I could not move past the point of believing that those among us who can't take care of themselves need to be in the custody of a guardian, or in a quality-care facility; that those who are contagiously ill should be quarantined; and that those who cannot obey the law should be imprisoned. And that the rest of us should be out exercising our right to life, liberty, and the pursuit of happiness - not under the government's thumb. And that analogy left me feeling awfully prejudiced.

Daddy always said, "If the shoe fits, wear it." But just as I was ready to lace up my mean biased spirit and walk away in disgrace, the government unveiled more damaging affirmative action - forbidding discrimination on the basis of family status. And I just had to take another stab at getting my family and friends to see the light.

When the government started pitching kids against crotchety old grandmas and grandpas, mom and dads stepped up to the plate. And it appeared as though "family status" was going to hit the winning home run. But in the final analysis, the game was an All-American loss, with the government winning by a landslide.

Like all government causes, this one had a zillion pages of regulations, and some mighty far-reaching effects. All adult communities were banned. Elderly residents were required to live beside and rent to kids, unless of course they were decrepit enough to require government-dictated special care and handicapped facilities. Property owners lost the right to decide who moved into their houses. And new guidelines for both the construction and installation industries were born. Advertisements reading "no children" were stricken from newspaper ads everywhere, along with other restrictive verbiage. And the exact language allowed was passed down by the Feds. To be sure the law was implemented properly and obeyed throughout the land, real estate agents fell under new, more extensive guidelines. Government-subsidized housing, at the taxpayer's expense, was made available to families with children, so long as they were willing to move into communities and housing complexes previously reserved for adults. And instead of planting flowers, and passing the knowledge of freedom on to the next generation of Rotary Club members, many healthy senior citizens started fighting child vandalism. Once again, taxpayers footed the bill, and freedoms too numerous to count faded away.

As our leaders advocate taking more of our freedoms for the good of all, passing more laws for our protection, and launching more social programs that appear to eradicate the classes, just remember - history clearly shows that, in the process of creating a perfect socialistic society, only the government gets big and rich. And all the ordinary people become equally oppressed.

Have you noticed that, while appearing to eradicate the underclasses, our social programs have actually widened the gaps between us and spread the fear that separates us? My grandmother used to feed every bum who occasionally appeared on her kitchen stoop. Today more bums are appearing than ever before, but we are afraid to open our doors to feed them.

Did you ever notice that the only issues government is "pro-choice" on are abortion, homosexuality, and criminal rights; that all their affirmative action programs promote adversity between races and families; and that when government does stand up for individual rights, it is only for those who cannot oppose them, and always at the expense of the majority who can?

Why? Because the least capable resist little, settle for less, and pose no real threat to the government. Homosexuals and abortionists don't exactly mass produce a new generation of free thinkers. Criminals can be easily sanctioned to the detriment of mainstream society today, and justifiably locked up if they get out of line tomorrow. The diseased spread their illness, and then die off. No amount of help will enable the severely handicapped or decrepit elderly to rise up in protest. Dysfunctional families cannot unite for any cause. And citizens, segmented into small groups with adverse interests, never gain enough united strength to overcome.

The more we look at affirmative action, the more evident government's ploys become. Leaders use every disadvantaged cause they can think of, and get us to buy into, as an excuse to gain power and wealth - and "reverse discrimination" is their main tool. Reverse discrimination is the excuse leaders use to perpetuate over half this massive bureaucracy we support. Just imagine the number of government agencies that would disappear if we didn't have to be protected against each other's prejudices and discriminations.

Surely we, who are capable of landing on the moon and communicating with Mars, can find a way to care for our disadvantaged and deal fairly with each other without relying on government. Forfeiture of our rights to the government gave us slavery and war in the first place. Then it gave us quotas in reverse, instead of equal rights for all. And now, under the guise of affirmative action, the red, white, and blue is turning into some mighty frightening colors - races all dangling on a brown rope too short to reach true equality, religion in a black closet, fading blue families, streets and schools filled with bloody red violence, subverted gray sexes, healthy pinks sacrificed for the sake of weak pale yellow, and gold flowing into the hands of a few greedy bold leaders.

Remember - real freedom and equality doesn't stir hate and fear; it replaces it with respect. Real freedom and equality isn't about conceding our rights to someone else, and appearing to all be the same; it's about all having rights and being individuals. Real freedom and equality doesn't force men and women to take from each other, or require anyone to give up what they've earned by the sweat of their brow; it allows all the opportunity to be the best they can be, and inspires us to share as much as we can afford. Real freedom and equality isn't about being protected by government; it's about being able to think and decide for oneself, and enjoying or dealing with the consequences of one's own decisions. Government quotas do not create real freedom and equality; they deny it.

Silent acceptance and a divided people are dangerous enemies of a free society. Our forefathers showed us the way to preserve freedom and turn it into opportunity. Today, we stand at the crossroads, with only two choices - broaden that freedom to include true liberty and equality for all, or watch it die as we further divide. When tough choices have to be made, we all have to stand up and be counted - even you and I.

Remember - as the rights of the majority go, so go the rights of everybody else in the country, and when the majority loses their individual freedoms, nobody will be free.

Remembering Foreign Policy

As the names on the Vietnam Memorial rolled by on the TV screen, my mind wandered back to the days when we watched thousands of our boys come home in flag-draped body bags and boxes. That was back when our government spared the enemy, at the expense of our own guys; back when our Youth protested in the streets at home, while Congress denied them the military strength needed to win over there; and back when too many of us fell silent, while our representatives in Washington started promoting themselves to a position of world leadership.

Then we started going to war in accordance with the United Nations. That saved some American lives, initially anyway. But U.N. results still seem too similar to our own - moving from one expensive conflict to another, without resolving anything. With the U.N., we buzzed into Iraq to the tune of trillions of American dollars and all our military might, and won the war hands down. But the threat rages on. That defeated dictator is still in place, and still calling the shots. From underground, with over five million American dollars in his pocket, Hussein is still hiding enough power to threaten the world with war again - while Iraqi refugees still starve.

Don't you get tired of spending American lives and dollars on these little tyrants? Even the ones who may be nice enough to take care of their people, and sell us oil today, usually change their minds tomorrow. Like Kuwait and Saudi Arabia, they all have two classes of people - the poor and the wealthy heads of state. They are filthy rich regimes, with leaders who line their mansions with gold rugs, and still behead any hungry person who dares speak out against them.

When we went to war to protect that dictator in Kuwait, my thoughts went back to the day we ousted Batista from Cuba and empowered Fidel Castro to take his place. You do remember Castro? He's that communist we put in power for the good of the Cuban people some years back - the one with nuclear missiles just ninety miles off our shores. Remember when he brought us to the brink of World War III, back in the sixties? And remember all those dissidents and criminals he's been putting out to sea in row boats ever since? And all that applause over his eloquent speeches up there in New York was for what? Oh yes - the Pope's descension from Rome and a celebration of Christmas, after thirty-five years of reigning terror. And you want to hear it for Castro again?

Remember when the U.N. rushed in to bring peace and prosperity to Bosnia? You saw the starving and homeless on television, trudging through the mud and rain, dragging naked kids behind them. Those pictures were priceless. They bought a twenty billion dollar peace accord in Dayton, Ohio, a catered vacation for the scoundrels who started that muddy war, and a trickle of cargo planes dropping just enough food to inspire the hungry to fight more. But that's okay. We only lost a few American lives, and only by accident. And although we don't hear much about it anymore, our troops are still at risk there. Our dollars are still being pilfered - some by their crooks, and some by our own. And the ordinary people of Bosnia are still just as hungry and homeless.

But we got distracted. The reign of war we fought and won for peace in the Mid East got more of our kids blown up in Saudi Arabia. Rumors of Hussein's chemical war threats made global headlines. And the United Nations started negotiating a peaceful resolution to the conflict between that threatening Iraqi dictator and a seemingly-vindictive United States. Naturally the Russians, our newest freeloading friends in outer space, sided with Iraq.

Those Russians have become real lovers of peace and freedom, you know - so much so that they sold twelve billion dollars worth of surplus weapons to Hussein. It kind of reminded me of Oliver North - the guy who used to sell extra American weapons to Iran, back when the Iranians were in the business of hijacking airplanes and holding American passengers hostage.

And speaking of foreign policy changes, Yasir Arafat is back - crusading for peace in the Middle East again. Remember the man who openly celebrated his title as head terrorist for the Palestine Liberation Organization (PLO), back in the seventies. As he recently rubbed shoulders with our leaders on the steps of the White House, I thought about our boys lying dead in the streets of Beirut. When Clinton congratulated and thanked Arafat for past decades of great Palestinian leadership, I couldn't believe my ears. Apparently our President has forgotten that we sent our boys in, without bullets in their guns, to keep the peace where Arafat was making war, and that Arafat's terrorists shot them down. Remember? Ah yes, people change. Sure Arafat is still head of the PLO. But he's a nicer, more soft-spoken, less radical terrorist now. According to his latest speech, he advocates "violent terrorism" only as a last resort.

We certainly understand that. We've always been a kinder gentler nation. We rebuilt the Japanese economy after World War II, and let them buy American land with the profits. When some of our citizens were trying to free their families from Castro's clutches, our soldier boys stationed in Guantanamo Bay remained neutral. Under the direction of the United Nations, Americans give the world all the respect it deserves. The largest portion of our national debt is an obligation to the U.N., but we still support member countries individually, just to keep down the threat of nuclear war. We perpetuate the world trade efforts of every derelict country around. And since we're no longer a nation of Christians, who believe that Jesus Christ is King of the Jews, we don't side with Israel that much anymore. We finally understand that all those thousands of lives lost during World War II, and the billions of dollars in aid ever since, wasn't supposed to protect an Israeli nation - it was to keep Germany from getting all that oil, and to enable Japan to compete with us in the world marketplace.

And speaking of world marketplaces - Americans are now sponsoring Mexico's right to free trade. In order to ease the flow of drugs into the U.S., and to curb their use of child labor, we purchased Mexican strawberries for our federal school lunch program. Sure Mexican strawberries were cheaper, but shipping ate up the savings that could have been passed on to American taxpayers. Sure we sold American strawberry farmers down the tubes; that's why fresh home-grown berries cost us more. And yes, too many American kids had to be given shots for Hepatitis A, because too many Mexican strawberries were infectious. But President Clinton made things right, with his new five-point food safety program. He gave forty three million taxpayer dollars to countries who want to export better quality foods, and the Federal Food and Drug Administration (FDA) more power to regulate what Americans eat.

While kids in Michigan were still recuperating from Mexico's poison strawberry festival, our President and Vice President took their families to China - to negotiate on our behalf. Yes, China is still a major communist bloc. And yes, she still proudly supports our enemies, openly commits horrible atrocities against her own people, and refuses to lay down her nuclear arms. But our President saw fit to give her enough nuclear capabilities to fry our potatoes anyway. And as our leaders returned, with the bill for their trips, American taxpayers rewarded their humanitarian efforts with another new trade agreement by which to fill the hope chests of our children with more products labeled "made in China."

But there's a bright side - if we're lucky, the Chinese won't destroy their own best marketplace. And as our stock market takes an occasional roller coaster ride, in the midst of a prospering economy at home, the United Nations says it will only take two hundred billion dollars to keep it on track - just enough to bail out the world's banks and spare Indonesia, China, Japan, North and South Korea, and our dear friends in Vietnam from bankruptcy. Our President agrees. Like Arafat, Clinton is improving. He's taken it upon himself to bomb foreign terrorists behind the backs of our elected representatives, just as secretly as he moves in on the young women we employ.

Let's get real here. While we sit idly by, content in the belief that America is still the world's haven, our leaders sacrifice us. We die trying to preserve foreign liberty, but the people we fight for are never free. We give billions to provide for foreign needy, but the world's hungry never get fed.

We see poverty-stricken women and children dodging bombs and bullets on the national news. And if we don't agree to pay, we face the threat of watching our boys die right alongside theirs. So we pick up the tab for negotiations and compromise, while our Presidents and their dictators roll out red carpets for each other. They trade our wealth and favors, while we forge on with the rest of the world's masses in martyrdom. Some treaties get signed, and a few cargo planes of food trickle in to hungry people who seldom eat. Then the leaders fly home in big private jets, and ride to their mansions in chauffeured limousines - satisfied for the moment with the peace we've purchased with our lives. The dictator left in control over there disappears into luxurious seclusion, his people too drained to be worth leading. He'll lie low, at least until our money runs out, while all his starving followers roam homelessly in squalor.

Meanwhile, because we still have something left to give, we hear and see a lot from our leader. Our President comes home smiling, and takes center stage, making the speeches that will inspire us to feel responsible and guilty enough to give more than he's already committed to pay. His humbling rhetoric is always the same: it starts out with, "I'm so glad to be back in the land of plenty, and so proud to ask the people of the wealthiest nation on earth to feed the poor we left behind." But once he's sure we've been properly indoctrinated to pay, without throwing him out of office or staging another Boston Tea Party, he changes his tune to a subtle threat of war: "We must preserve this fragile restless peace."

As soon as we've been properly groomed to pay for the next uprising, that old dictator comes out of the closet again, ranting indignantly about American's warring capitalists. By then he's running low on funds, and some of his people have gained a little strength, or gotten big enough to tote a gun. So with loads of misguided compassion, misplaced guilt, and a knapsack full of bills from the last round, we rush dollars and lives back to the front lines again.

Aren't you sick of the same old bull, and the idiocy that follows? Whether we win the war or not, we eagerly strengthen our enemies. We feed and arm them, both before and after war, knowing full well they will rise to do us harm on another day. We fight the same old battles, and foot the same old bills, for the same atrocities of the same old tyrants, over and over again. And we even take their ridicule as we do it.

If we are truly interested in the survival of our nation, if we truly believe in the preservation of freedom everywhere, and if we really want to meet the needs of those less fortunate in the world, we must draw up new guidelines for sharing and going to war. We must be more realistic about what we can afford to do, when to do it, and for whom we do it. And we may even want to establish a new agenda for those we entrust to handle our deliveries.

Of course making these kinds of changes present some real mental challenges. Are we up to the task? Not according to those who would stifle us. Granted, we may not be well versed on foreign policy, and they'd like us to believe it's too complicated for ordinary thinkers. But our simple-minded logic is obviously more sensible than anything the current decision makers have come up with.

It's time we sent Washington, and the world, a strong message - one that will assure ordinary people everywhere that we are united and firmly embedded in freedom. We need to let them know that we intend to preserve liberty and justice for ordinary people at home first, then abroad - only where people really want and need it. It's time to write your congressman some new foreign policy guidelines.

Whether it be in self defense, to fight aggression, to save

humanity, or plain old self preservation and greed, we the people should demand the right to decide how much of our money and how many of our lives any foreign conflict is worth. We want to know the truth before we give, or go to war. And any government official found guilty of deceiving the American people should be immediately impeached.

Put American interests first. Tolerate no more trade agreements with foreign governments that are not equally beneficial to the United States. Tolerate no leader who sleeps with enemies that poison our children, stifles our economy, supports our enemies, and snuffs the life from our soldiers.

Provide no more aid to foreign governments who blatantly flaunt and perpetuate war and threaten the world's peoples. Support no country with a dictator who commits atrocities against his own people, unless he concedes enough openness and control to verify that our money and goods actually reach the people we intend to help.

Provide no more aid or military assistance to people who stone and ridicule our soldiers. Riots against us in foreign streets indicate that the ordinary people don't want us there, any more than we want to be there, and that leaders from both sides are forcing the situation on all of us. We wouldn't like it if the armies and monies from another country marched in to change our way of life or decide our fate. And we have enough sense to know that we should stay home when we aren't welcome elsewhere. According to our own principles of independence, company gets an invitation, and any other intruder is guilty of trespassing - surely we can respect others no less. And if we are really war mongers, let's muster the gall to admit it. That's the only way to force our leaders to bring the captured bounties home. If we're going to foot the bill, we might as well share the wealth.

Let's instruct our leaders never to relinquish control of our military to the United Nations or any other foreign power without the consent of the American people. And forget the perpetuation of a global economy for now. We know we cannot withdraw from the world, but we must not be content to let the United Nations dictate our economic or military plight. Too many of its members are not of a democratic nature. Too many take advantage of our resources. Too many withhold support for U.S. troops at risk while assisting our enemies.

We are not interested in saving the dignity of a foreign dictatorship. As we grieved with the families of those soldiers killed in that Saudi bombing, our leaders concentrated on preserving Saudi dignity. And the culprits, who made and delivered the bomb that blew up our kids, were never brought to justice. When a news reporter mentioned that the limitations put on us by the Saudi government may have jeopardized the safety of our sons and daughters there, we didn't even bring the remaining soldiers home - we just left them at risk in that foreign land. No more of that.

All our military might must be behind any American soldier sent into any foreign danger zone. Not one American life should be sacrificed without a full commitment of everything available to support our troops - including the full cooperation of the regime where they reside.

Let the world know that every time we risk our lives, we intend to win the war. And when we win, we intend to act like victors. If the cause is worth the lives of our sons and daughters, the enemy regime must be destroyed, and the land must be restored as a part of our democracy. No more having to die fighting the same old battles and tyrants, to save the same people from starvation over and over again.

When foreign enemies realize that America no longer puts world interests ahead of the well being of its own people, they'll find somebody else with whom to pick their fights. Only then will American citizens, and anyone else they are willing to fight for, finally live in peace - prosperously, safely, and freely.

WHO'S WHO IN AMERICA

I was born along the Ohio River, and lived there most of my life. I've never been arrested, or committed any serious infraction against society that I know of. Yet to get a real estate license in Ohio, I had to take four courses at the college level, and prove I was fit to deal with the public. When I moved and established legal residency in Florida, I had to be finger-printed and pass a background check to work in the public schools. And to sell real estate, I had to be finger-printed again, pass another character and background check, and take a rigorous state exam to prove my competency. We bought a home seven years before my children graduated from high school. My youngest son earned numerous awards and scholarships, including "Christian Athlctc" during his scnior ycar. But wc practically had to produce our life story, and at least eleven documents proving residency, before he could qualify for in-state tuition - and we were U. S. citizens earning and paying our own way.

Yet Pedro Medina was welcomed into this country, and into the state of Florida, with open arms. A welfare check, and all the opportunity for education and employment he wanted awaited him. We taxpayers supported him during his long stay here - mostly in prison. And we provided him years of legal defense. Finally, Medina died in Florida's electric chair, for torturing and stabbing a young girl to death.

When it is easier for a foreign criminal to get into the United States than it is for law-abiding U.S citizens to move from one state to another, do business in their home states, and get into their own universities, we know we have to make some changes. I know America has always been the world's haven. But today we are going to have to be more practical when it comes to immigration and foreign travelers.

Given the increased acts of international terrorism, the black marketing of arms, drug-based foreign economies exporting to the U.S., the endless stream of foreign criminals coming into our country, and the overwhelming needs of our own people which aren't being met, the United States has no choice but to secure and close her borders - at least until we can identify, protect, and meet the needs of our own people.

I know the government says it's doing the best it can. But its best isn't working. A staggering percentage of our soaring crime rate is attributed to noncitizens. As Congress approved Clinton's multi-billion dollar task force to study and clean up crime in South America, thousands more illegal immigrants from eight different countries poured across our southern borders. As American cops sipped coffee with Juan Valdez, Columbia shipped us eighty percent of the cocaine we found on our streets yesterday. As we made trade concessions to boost the Mexican economy, and our government fed their poison strawberries to our school children, Mexico dropped its best marijuana crop on our doorstep. And drug-related violent crimes rose another seventeen percent. As two hundred thousand of our teenagers entered drug rehabilitation centers, and hundreds more died of overdoses on our streets, our elected representatives increased aid to countries with drug-based economies.

President Clinton and Congress believe that, if we pay these drug pushers enough, they'll sit on their duffs instead of harvesting intoxicating crops for sale to the U.S. But Clinton and those other elected representatives who support his policies are wrong. Foreign drug pushers are buying our land with the money we give them, and setting up illegal pharmacies along the edges of our city streets -

right near all the stoned Americans who are sleeping in cardboard boxes. And we must stop them.

If the Red Chinese can secure their borders, given all the high tech equipment and computer systems we have, so can we. Tougher standards for applicants and better scrutiny of passport credentials shouldn't be any harder for our government than it is for theirs. But we might want to be a little pickier about who we let in. Al Gore got in to tour the Great Wall of China - and the last I heard, he was an American agent accused of money laundering.

Besides, American businesses are already using the perfect screening device -that little gadget that buzzes when you leave a local department store without paying for the dress you're taking out the door. An immigrant, with enough money to pay for his gadget, could buzz his way right through border check points. And if he couldn't afford to pay, we'd know to give him a cell with all the comforts of home - before he got a chance to hurt anybody.

Seriously, we have satellites that can pick out a toad from outer space. And we have mechanisms that can see cars through concrete bridges after dark. You'd think we could spot an illegal immigrant anytime, anyplace, and in anything. We have check points at most air and sea entrances, and only a few hundred miles of land crossings to protect. If we're short on manpower, we can always assign more law enforcement agents to the border patrol -perhaps a few of those policemen we see doubled up and blocking traffic around highway fender benders. And instead of playing hide and seek with those crossing the boarder illegally, officers need to start shooting. Believe me, this problem is not a game.

Our resources are limited and dwindling. Our environment is deteriorating, our prisons are overflowing, and we cannot keep up with the needs of our own hungry and homeless. As we cleaned up the mess from the World Trade Center bombing, thousands of foreign students filled the seats of our medical schools. As our young battled terrorism in the Middle East, our homeless and sick streamed into inner city war zones. As we freely deliver the babies of illegal immigrants, and make them immediate citizens eligible for welfare, too many of our own go without food, clothing, and medicine. As we subsidize the sale of our assets to foreigners, future generations of Americans inherit a huge trade deficit. As we continue to neglect our own needy, and fail to safeguard our own future, our kids are fast becoming the most-endangered species on earth.

My Dad always said, "Charity begins at home," and most people would agree with him. In fact, I don't know of anybody on earth, except Americans, who willingly provide so much for so many outsiders, while letting their own go hungry and homeless in a hostile environment. If we are to survive as a free and prosperous nation, we must take care of our own. We must halt immigration before too many more of our own people become street refugees.

I'm not suggesting that we stop sharing. I know some of you have poor families, who are not citizens, living both here and abroad; and I know they need your help. Feel free to send them all you can afford. Just remember - my mother is a citizen, born and living here. And she needs my help. I can't afford to support the needy in my family and yours too. And in good conscience, I can't feed your mother while watching mine go hungry. So please don't ask me to. My free haven can no longer afford the taxing abuse.

When we suggested cutting expenses to balance the budget, leaders increased aid to foreigners, while cutting Medicare and welfare to elderly and needy Americans. Maybe the guys we entrust to handle our affairs can't distinguish aliens from U. S. citizens. Maybe it's time we, who elect them to office and pay their salaries, taught them to tell the difference.

Demanding that all official forms be in English, and adding the designation "U.S. Citizen" to them, would help. We are required to have plenty of documentation to back up our existence, and it's all kept on file in some government office, somewhere. We have birth certificates, Social Security cards, medical records, driver's licenses, school records, military draft registrations, voter registrations, property and income tax records. Government permits, and licenses are required for just about everything we do. How 'bout requiring noncitizens to produce that much documentation before allowing them to do or have anything here?

Someone suggested that we relieve the Internal Revenue Service (IRS) of its duty to collect taxes, rename it Illegal Resident Supervisors (IRS), and assign it new responsibilities - finding illegal aliens and rendering them harmless. That makes sense. After all, the IRS already has a list of everybody who has paid taxes, still owes, or is not of the right age to pay. And they know everyone else is a foreigner. Besides that, the IRS knows where everybody lives, what everybody has, and how to get their hands on all our possessions. If the IRS could freeze and confiscate the assets of criminal aliens, just like they do ours when we forget to file our tax returns, these social menaces would soon be doing business someplace else. And imagine the relief we'd feel - government oppression directed toward real culprits instead of at free Americans, a measure of justice supported by ill-gotten gain instead of our pay checks, and two groups of criminals prohibited from harassing American citizens.

Speaking of harassing good citizens - we need to fix that too. Our governing bodies have handed us twenty-six thousand new gun regulations, while allowing ten billion dollars worth of illegal weapons to be smuggled into our country by foreigners. While we are being jailed for driving under the influence, drunken foreign diplomats freely speed around town. And while our cars are being impounded, we are paying for theirs. While Americans are arrested for endangering the lives of children not fastened in car seats properly, these drunken diplomats get immunity for running down our kids. Diplomatic immunity may be necessary under certain circumstances. But for the most part, it is nothing more than a sweet little niche created by those in power, to give themselves privilege over the rest of us. I say we limit it severely. If a deed is perilous enough to stifle American liberty, it's perilous enough to warrant the stifling of foreigners too.

Everyone in the United States today is either here as an American citizen or as a foreigner. And granted, when you live in a multinational country like ours, it is a little difficult to tell who is which. Our physical characteristics are a mixture from every corner of the globe, and we all add our personal accents to the language. But since visitors and illegal aliens act differently than citizens do, I suggest we start identifying people by their deeds.

Americans are out there protecting our freedoms, and sharing our responsibilities, as well as our successes. They speak our language, even if it is with an accent. They respect our laws and traditions, and understand the use of our manners. Even if they're new or handicapped, they try - and the rest of us can help them. Citizens who can't take care of themselves are in the custody of a guardian, or in a quality care facility. And the ones who can't obey the law are in jail.

Foreigners within our boundaries are either here as criminal aliens or as legal visitors just passing through. Legal visitors are vacationing, or tending to official business. And except for being friendly hosts, we don't have to be too concerned with them, so long as they are screened properly before entering, and abide by our laws while they're here.

Just being here illegally is a crime, and foreigners who do not obey our laws are criminal aliens. Recognizing these enemies of our society can be as difficult as dealing with them once they're caught. They lie, and try to disguise themselves as citizens. And when we catch them, they put us on guilt trips, or threaten us with war-like retaliation - saying things like, "You wealthy capitalists will pay with the lives of your sons." These people are easy to spot. They rob our businesses instead of getting jobs. They teach their children to vandalize our neighborhoods instead of sending them to school. They demand our food, and then bite our hand as we feed them. And they are rude. They call us nasty names behind our backs, in a language we cannot understand. They push and shove, and run us down with grocery carts, just to be the first in line to spend state welfare checks. They use counterfeit documents, and smuggle drugs too.

These offenders are a serious threat to our society. And we shouldn't keep them here - unless they're being punished or awaiting deportation. As soon as they are caught, they should be searched and stripped of all possessions gathered in America, forced to make quick monetary restitution whenever possible, then escorted to the nearest harbor for immediate deportation - hopefully at their own expense. And if they cause injury or devastation to one of ours, that's severe enough to warrant punishment here, the maximum penalty under our law should be mandated, and swift in coming.

Once the playing field is leveled to those who are willing to share the responsibilities of freedom, as well as the wealth of opportunity, it shouldn't take us long to get back on our feet and reopen our borders. But before reopening, we must devise a workable system for screening and barring those who would do us harm - one that accents catching intruders, not stifling our own freedom. Those coming into America must be able to identify themselves fully and document their legitimate right to be here, just like we have to do. They must be willing and able to abide by the laws of our land. And they must be capable of supporting themselves, or have families here that can and will take care of them.

Before we reclaim our place as world providers, we must take a little time out to bring balance and common sense back into our own society. We must do our part to heal ourselves here at home before we take on the rest of the world again.

Badgering Bad Agents

During the course of doing business this week, I witnessed daily violations of every professional licensing law of the land. While driving down the freeway at the posted speed limit, other motorists flew past me like I was sitting still. And I saw too many rules being broken all along the way. People were indifferent to the needs of each other, and disrespect for fellow human beings was overly apparent everywhere I stopped. In the Walmart parking lot, drivers and pedestrians were clashing over who had the right-of-way. Everybody stood stomping and complaining, unwilling to let the other go first. A man shook his fists as I ran a new stop sign that I was too engrossed in the confusion to notice.

"We can't all be this bad, or this misguided in our thinking," I whispered under my breath. We are not mean spirited, or thoughtless juveniles. And the majority of us are not law breakers, nor criminals. So why do so many good people, in a free society, show such blatant disrespect for each other and for the laws of their land?

Maybe we doubt the leaders we've elected. After all, rumors about drugs, murder, sexual assault, and campaign-fund swindling surround our President. The media accuses the Vice President of laundering money and selling out to foreign interests. The Speaker of the House, along with several other judges and congressmen, have been disciplined for immoral and unethical conduct. Numerous scandals at every level of government abound. The President just admitted to lying, and has been impeached.

How can we expect to be a moral, law abiding country if a bunch of immoral crooks are running the show?

Maybe we've lost respect for too many law enforcement agencies and officers. After all, we witness more and more examples of police brutality and inadequacy every day. Even judges are being labeled incompetent. Our military instructors and officers are accused of numerous sexual assaults. And now, for our own protection, we women are being told to drive to a populated area before pulling over for a cop. Lawmen have a lot of nerve trying to make us behave when there's so much cleaning up to be done in their own back yards.

Maybe we doubt the integrity of the law. We're overwhelmed with confusing and unfair regulations that bog us down in courtroom debates and cost us hundreds of dollars per hour. Whether we are guilty or innocent, and whether we win or lose, we end up weary and wiped out financially by attorneys. Wonder why? Maybe it's because most of our legislature is made up of lawyers. And the more laws they give us to break and the more reasons they give us to sue each other, the more money they make. Nobody in their right mind obeys senseless laws written by leaders with a personal agenda for money and power.

Maybe we all smell rats. Today our leaders condone assisted suicide, call the murder of an ill and aged spouse "mercy killing," support the abortion of unwanted babies, and provide prisoners the opportunity to run business scams right from their cells. They provide those unable to rise up against them everything, from food and shelter to college educations, the best medical care, a well equipped gym, a big screen TV, and free rides everywhere - while the most capable among us are taxed and regulated to death. No wonder being a capable, honest, hard working adult isn't too popular anymore.

There are no maybes about it. All of the above are true. And those truths are being reflected throughout our society-in the attitudes and actions of its members. Maybe we're not the bad guys here. But when leaders act like gangsters and morons, only shysters and idiots follow. And humans tend to act the way they are treated. The more laws aimed at coddling dummies and babies, the more ignorant and infantile we became. When juvenile confusion breeds enough apathy and disrespect, the nation turns to blatant disobedience and social decay. And when we appear too lame to look out for ourselves, too mentally demented to distinguish right from wrong, and too incapable of making good value judgements, our leaders will gladly do it for us. Are we there yet? I think we're close.

Remember - disrespect and repeated violations will not bring back freedom and continued prosperity, any more than sticking our heads in the sand brought law and order. To clean up the mess, we're going to have to change things- and that may mean getting rid of the bad leaders and officials who are causing the decay.

Because our Constitution guarantees every American citizen freedom of religion and definitely mandates the separation of church and state, our Congress banned our right to pray in public schools. Yet they turned right around and designated a National Day of Prayer. I don't know about you, but I needed that day on my knees before God - asking for deliverance from an oppressive government that denies freedom to worship out of one side of its face, while designating a time to pray out of the other. As Daddy used to say, "Jesus Christ wasn't suggesting that we be two-faced when he instructed us to turn the other cheek." But then too many of our elected representatives are neither Biblically nor Constitutionally inspired to uphold the highest laws of our land. And we have only to look across the street to find further evidence of the disrespect these leaders show for the rights of American citizens.

The other night a news commentator reported that the city of Orlando was banning dancing after midnight, and enforcing a twelve o'clock curfew throughout the nightclub area downtown - because of suspected drug use at late night dances. Now I'm past fifty years old, and the last thing I want to do is dance all night. However, since dancing is a perfectly legal activity, and this is a free country, I expect to be allowed to do it if I so choose.

I admit that a lot of the participants at those dances were young people. But few, if any of them, were minors. And I'm not real comfortable with the government establishing curfews for adults. Besides, the city's own statistics confirmed that nine out of ten young adults in attendance were not doing drugs. Now I know one's too many, but taking away the rights of nine innocent people won't stop one crime anywhere. And isn't it curious - the people we pay to protect us from crime were close enough to see and count the criminals. But instead of arresting the bad guys, they threatened to arrest and fine innocent people for staying out too late.

Today our government announced that Americans are spending fifty seven billion dollars on illegal drugs. And they can tell you which per cent of which kind comes from which foreign country. Again - they are there to count the money and identify the crooks, but can't make the arrests or hand out the punishments that could stop the crime.

Are the people we pay to curb social decay just incompetent? Or are they interested in using the ugly statistics to justify empowering themselves against us? Maybe they're on the take, and need to stay in power to keep their pockets lined. Again, probably all of the above are true. But no matter. We must get rid of them - both those who feather their nests by selling out freedom, and those too depraved to know any better.

If we are to function together in a civilized fashion, we must have guidelines to follow. But they must come from competent, moral people. And too many of the guys we have making and enforcing our laws seem to be neither. While they're investigating perfectly normal business activities, and doing nothing to stop crime, even people as public as the Clintons may be getting away with murder - perhaps even serial killing, according to the press.

When rumors of Hillary's affairs started surfacing, they said her boyfriend accidently drowned. Whitewater partner (Vince Foster) committed suicide. And then some guy died in a car wreck - supposedly after finding cancelled checks in Foster's car that were written to people the Clintons claimed they hadn't paid off. When McDougal died in prison, reporters said he'd been deliberately denied medical treatment. After Ron Brown's airplane crashed, they said he was about to expose Clinton's scheme to sell big business a ride on trade agreement missions. And that Arkansas state policeman who escorted Paula Jones to Bill's hotel conveniently got run over by a truck. These are a lot of unfortunate circumstances. It appears as though this President leaves as many mysterious deaths in his wake as he does sexual encounters.

If the Clintons are innocent, having hundreds of investigators accusing them and staying hot on their trail publicly for six years, without ever uncovering enough evidence to warrant an arrest is not a just pursuit - it's an invasion of privacy, harassment, and slander. And whether you're Joe-citizen or the President, no American should have to endure that. However, if they are guilty, and have been able to survive this long, without even being charged, every American is at risk.

Taking twenty years to find a unibomber who's operating from inside some secluded forest is bad enough. But given the amount we pay investigators, as many as we have on the payroll, and as much high-tech equipment as we provide them to work with, you'd think they be able to tell when there was any funny business with figures as public as the Clintons. These scandals involving Clinton and other prominent public servants make it obvious that some of our agents can't be trusted to do a good job. The question is which ones - the President, the staff, our representatives, the investigators, the prosecutors, or all of them?

Someone said the majority of Americans are too busy to care whether or not their representatives and public servants are doing a good job. And as tradition would have it, some of us don't pay much attention until something goes wrong. Well, today some things are going wrong, and we need to sit up and take notice.

The bad guys we've elected aren't being honest with us. Remember the ones who bought poison Mexican strawberries with our tax dollars and fed them to our school children? Some of them frequent the finest hotels with those who would destroy us, and make secret pacts to sell arms to our enemies. Some even drop bombs without Congressional consent. Some conduct private investigations and harass innocent citizens, while others hold secret meetings and then shred all the records so we can't prove their dirty dealings. A few reduce our employees to whores, make a mockery of the affirmative action laws they hold us to, and blow semen around in the offices we pay for. Others collect trillions of our dollars to control crime and stop poverty in America, but never get the job done. Most collect taxes under false pretenses, and never provide us an accurate accounting. Many lie. And they all know better.

Speaking of knowing better - do we really want an illiterate president? If Clinton doesn't know the meaning of the word "alone" and he doesn't know what having a sexual relationship means, can we entrust him to communicate our wants and needs around the world - or should we replace him with a fifth grader?

Don't kid yourself - our elected representatives know how to behave. They even know how to be good agents. They wrote the book on "Laws of Agency". That rule book tells all about how good agents should behave, and helps everyone understand how damaging a bad agent can be. American citizens are held to those laws when they act as real estate agents, trustees, guardians, executors of estates, and all the other situations where they serve as agents for one another - even when representing a friend or family member, or agreeing to serve without pay.

According to agency laws, if you agree to represent another person, for any legal purpose, you are the "fiduciary agent" of that person. And as such, you are required to be trustworthy and honest with the person you represent. You are required to maintain their confidentiality, and always act in their best interest. There are strict rules for collecting, disbursing and accounting for a client's money - so it is not misused or mixed up with an agent's personal funds. And serving or representing anyone for any illegal purpose, or in any illegal way, is a violation of those agency laws.

Laws that define an agency relationship are made quite clear - so clear in fact that they inflict pretty severe penalties on those of us who fail to comply. Citizens who violate an agency relationship are subject to fine, imprisonment, loss of pay and privileges, revocation of licenses, immediate termination, and/or all of the above. On top of the criminal penalties, a citizen-agent is required to make restitution if he or she causes a client financial loss. And the agent can be sued for damages in civil court. But government leaders have somehow exempted themselves from all that.

Don't you think its time we started holding our elected and appointed representatives in government to the same high standards they set for us? It's time we got rid of bad agents, from the federal government all the way down to local law enforcement officers - whether they are out to deliberately stifle freedom, or just too ignorant to do their jobs. It's time we demanded that all government agents act in the best interest of their clients - we free American citizens. And if they don't, let's oust them - while we still have enough power left to vote and impeach.

Of course that'll bring us to the next problem - finding and recruiting new and better ones to take their place. Paying a fair wage, and demanding a job well done will get the ball rolling. But it won't be enough. The stifling volumes of rules and regulations we've inherited have left us all a little foggy about what freedom really means, and it's created a shortage of public servants who understand the principles on which our nation was founded. So we're going to have to put things on hold long enough to set up new guidelines, get some good people interested and involved, and maybe even train some young folks to help manage the country's affairs.

Take Back Control Of Your Kids

Today we all live in fear of crime, and far too many good people have been victims. We may be fed up enough to deal pretty harshly with adults. But what are we going to do to stop violence among the children?

After being robbed and beaten nine times, a decrepit old man from Deltona went out and purchased a gun. Late the next night, he shot and killed one of two boys breaking into his home. The police dragged over five thousand dollars worth of stolen merchandise from the deceased fourteen-year-old's bedroom. Instead of being charged, the sixteen-year-old accomplice was given a week off school, to grieve the loss of his friend. And the seventy-eight year old victim was arrested for murder. As both mothers sobbed about how older people should be more patient with kids, the community demanded more supervision. And another cry went up for government to intervene in the child-rearing process.

Think back to when you were fourteen or sixteen, and on the verge of adulthood. Remember how ready, willing and able you were - physically developed and capable of reproducing, able to drive a car, wise enough to count and spend money, even bright enough to keep house and get a job. And remember that irresistible inner drive to step out and experience the world on your own. Mother Nature was trying to tell you it was about time to cut the apron strings. And she didn't mean "switch custody to Uncle Sam" or any other watchful eye of the government. She still doesn't today.

Today teenagers are molesting and robbing old ladies. Ten-year-old kids are stabbing and shooting each other to death. Juvenile detention centers are overflowing. Kids are becoming so vicious that we must try them as adults. And if we raise another generation who relies so heavily on government instead of themselves, things will continue to worsen - until finally they'll have to take away all the rights our children have. When the government has all their toys, all their strength and will, all their adult guns, and all the power it needs to protect us against them, they will not be free.

In case you're doubting it - the majority of our kids can learn to be good, and are capable of growing up to be free. But preparing them to be grown-up starts the day they are born, and takes a whole childhood to complete. But when Mother Nature starts calling them into adulthood, they go-whichever way they've been programmed to. Unfortunately, many parents wait to long too start preparing their kids. Some unwittingly go about it the wrong way. And others neglect it altogether. Either way, most of us do the best we can. And only after it's too late do we realize where we made our mistakes.

But we can help each other. Unity is the greatest ally of free and decent people - and the worst nightmare for a controlling government. Ordinary people must get to know and trust each other again, reestablish faith in each other, develop respect and a human understanding for each other, and learn to rely on each other again. It's the only way to watch out for and raise the nations children.

I was visiting a friend of mine the other day. Her five-year-old son happened to be flicking back and forth between a couple's body massage on the Playboy channel and something horribly violent. I asked Jan if it was okay for him to be watching that stuff. She wasn't sure the material was fit for him to see, but didn't want to infringe on his right to choose. Falling back on the old philosophies from my generation, I protested, "He's too young to know what's good for him, and if you don't tell him, who will?" Obviously aggravated with my interference, she snapped, "There's nudity, sexual allure, and violence on with everything, from regular commercials to music and videos; and I can't shut him away from the whole world, you know." She reminded me of the days when Elvis could not be shown from the waist down on national television, and suggested that I was old fashioned. To preserve the friendship, we agreed to change the subject.

But the incident got me thinking; Jan and I hadn't understood each other. I'm from the old "tell it like it is and lay down the law" school. Jan shuns away from that, preferring to be more flexible and open-minded. She was concerned about what her son was watching, and she was looking for some insight. In fact, she started screening some of his selections after that, but could never admit she listened to "old-fashioned" me. And I truly cared, and meant only to help, not boss or interfere. But my tone and attitude must have been too arrogant to convey that message. If Jan and I could learn to communicate past the egos of our generation gap, Jan could help me understand and appreciate the valuable aspects of her new, more modern way of thinking. And I could share some old ideas that might still work for her today.

Wouldn't it be great if adults could realize that, whether new or old, almost everything has two elements in common-some value, and some room for improvement. And alterations can be made without throwing away the basic fabric of either one. Even the Constitution needs amending from time to time, but we still cling to its basic freedoms. Moral standards are no different. The Puritan notions and hickory sticks of past generations were far too harsh and restrictive. But a swing to little or no discipline has proven to be just as bad or worse.

How 'bout some balance between new and old? We must teach our kids to think responsibly and act independently. Whether we like it or not, this old world has not yet evolved into a rose garden. The negative repercussions they must learn to cope with and/or avoid have not evaporated. Free sex sounds great to those who prefer college to getting married young, but pregnancy and disease have not yet been eradicated. We'd better be sure our children know enough to engage safely, before we show and tell them how good sex feels. Seeing 18,000 murders a year on the big screen may not bother modern-day kids, but some old fashioned explanations might help them grasp enough of the pain and death behind the scenes to stop the killing.

When my daughter was born, Playtex nursers had just been invented. And I'd been programmed to bottle feed. When her first baby came, that daughter decided the breast was best - in spite of my objections. I spent two weeks, watching Susan nurse her new baby. She shared the warmth, the educational booklets, and an occasional turn at bottle feeding with me. My daughter showed me that, by coming together with enough respect to listen to each other and to think about each other's philosophies, we could enjoy sharing each other's experiences and learn from each other's insights. Its a great way to blend the good from both the new and old, and make both worlds a better place. Right now we have three or four living generations of ideas to sort through. So let's get started.

My kids were raised in what I call the lucky generation - right between the old and the new. There were enough disciplines and principles left over from my Mom and Dad's generation to keep them out of serious trouble. And the world was still safe enough to let them explore all the new options. Drugs and crime were in the air, but not running rampant everywhere. And when I erred, the government could yet be held at bay. But I still have many regrets. And I still worry.

Successfully preparing the next generation to take over has never been easy. But as young parents embark upon the task of raising their kids today, they face a world more complicated and more rapidly changing than ever before. Their little ones are getting wrong messages from everything they see and hear. Their teenagers are being pulled from the nest sooner, and in more dangerous directions. And we've allowed government to set the standards for their health, safety, and welfare, while forbidding parents to do otherwise with their kids. That is wrong. Instead of handing children over to government, we must prepare them to make extremely better choices - choices that will see them through to adulthood.

Modern parents seem too busy to discipline. And I understand. If I only saw my babies two hours after work each day, I wouldn't want to spend that precious time training and correcting either. Naturally the government, and every profit-making organization around, understands this dilemmas - they created it. Government has created the reasons families move in opposite directions. And they are right there continuing to perpetuate the separation - with more propaganda to motivate staying absent from home, more expensive services to keep parents working, more psychology books to overwhelm our minds, and more limitations on parental authority.

My sister took her six-year-old grandson shopping for a pair of badly needed shoes. He ran up and down store aisles, deliberately running into other shoppers and knocking items off the shelves. But he refused to try on any shoes. After talking until she was blue in the face, while he continued to misbehave, Nancy finally gave up and took him back home - all in a tizzy about having to send him to school wearing ill-fitting shoes. I asked why she hadn't taken him by the arm and swatted his bottom, if that's what it took to make him behave. "Oh, I couldn't do that," she exclaimed; "I'd have been arrested within seconds if I'd touched him."

Most people I know have given up their right to discipline their children because they're afraid of being falsely accused and arrested - and with good reason. This country now has more federal and state Human Resource Service (HRS) divisions than the world has children's homes. And the primary purpose of HRS is to investigate parents suspected of improprieties, not to protect kids.

A few years back, HRS improprieties were defined as serious abuse and neglect. Today they mean anything, from taking the wrong medication while pregnant (and I don't mean illegal drugs) to misjudging a situation that might cause accidental injury to a child. The penalty used to be loss of custody for a serious infraction against a child. Today it is being sued by your child, or jailed by the government for failing to prevent a kid from falling down. And while good conscientious parents are being overshadowed, or intimidated for human errors, real and repeat child abusers are free to maim and kill - because the system is too complicated for even the government to make it work.

I was managing a day-care center when I had my first run in with HRS. One of my best caretakers came to me with a badly-bruised little boy. She knew from previous experience that HRS would do nothing to protect him or his two brothers from immediate danger. and she knew that betraying their confidence would further endanger and isolate them. But the boy needed medical attention, and we had no legal choice but to file a report. That evening HRS knocked on the home's door, scolded the mother and stepfather, who denied the allegations, and left without taking the kids. Sure enough, at 7:30 the next morning, the boys were on our day-care stoop - burned, bruised, and more brutally beaten than they'd been the day before. A preliminary background check revealed that the family, fleeing similar charges, had moved four times during the previous eighteen months.

So why hadn't HRS run that simple background check, and been prepared to take protective custody before they knocked on that door? The agent assigned to our case was too busy making the quota necessary to stay on the government's payroll. That quota is based on the number of reports investigated, not the time spent doing a thorough job of solving one child's problem. Although ours turned out to be the only real case of child abuse reported that night, the agent had justified keeping his job by interrogating a list of twenty-one parents. But he was not required to take any action to protect a single child. Luckily, out of sixty-three supposedly abused kids, ours were the only three who needed protection.

Granted, child abuse exists. But abusers are either insane or criminals. And regardless of what you see and hear on the evening news, the majority of us do not fit into either category. Remember - the norm does not make headlines. We need to simplify the laws designed to protect children so that they are enforceable against true offenders. And we need to incarcerate or eliminate those unable to control their violent behavior. But we must not banish the rights and judgements of good parents because of the inadequacies of a few.

We are human beings, and this is not Utopia. Sometimes we have to choose between the lesser of two evils. And you had better believe that when the life of a child is at stake, the safest bet is not with the government. Remember - once government gets control, ordinary people go without. The government that denied that old man the right to protect himself and his property was not there to keep illegal firearms from the hands of neighborhood children. The government that forbid Nancy to discipline her grandson wasn't there to see that Josh got his shoes. The government that forced us to report Billy's abuse, and forbid us to tend to his wounds, was not there to protect or heal him. And the government that defines child abuse is not there to protect most endangered children. In fact, as tragic as it may be for some children, most of the parents who really abuse their kids have been reported repeatedly by the time you see their pictures on the evening news.

There is only one real solution for our nation's children- Mommy and/or Daddy, along with a strong extended-family unit. The vast majority of us are not child abusers. In fact, with few exceptions, there is no greater natural instinct than the beastly drive to protect and care for offspring. Are we less than animals? No - the human animal is more prone to spoil and indulge, than to hurt or deny its child. Adults, both young and old, must join together, and demand that the government relinquish control of our children. And unless there is strong evidence to the contrary, we must give parents and grandparents back the respect they deserve - for only good parenting will bring common sense back into the child-rearing process.

No stranger will ever understand, or do what it takes to help kids form the opinions and make the decisions that will lead to their success, independence, and true happiness-not schools, not the government, not churches, not day-care centers, nor any other private organization, and certainly not well-intentioned dimwitted friends who encourage family disruption and bad habits. Kids need the firm hand of loving parents and grandparents. That's why we feel sorry for orphans.

Once I worked in a store with a seventeen-year-old girl who thought her father and stepmother were terribly unfair. Naturally I sided with her, and offered her a way out - my house. When we went to pick up Debbie's clothes, several little brothers and sisters cried. Even her mean stepmother looked on the verge of tears. Her sad and irate father begged her not to go, but did not stand in her way. I put a roof over her head, gave her a ride to work every day, and bean soup to eat with the rest of us, until she could finish her last year of high school. Other than that, she was old enough to fend for herself. Yeah, right. Within a few weeks she turned eighteen, quit school, and moved in with her boyfriend. The last time I saw her (years ago), she was pregnant and moving back home. To this day I can only pray that Debbie and her family forgive me, and that God somehow blessed her life in spite of my ignorant attempt to do good.

Only after I faced the wrath of some all-knowing self-righteous adults who befriended my complaining teenager did I come to realize how much pain that kind of distrust and interference can cause. And that's the good part. If the condemned parent hasn't already laid the basic foundation necessary to see their teenager through those turbulent times, a young life can be destroyed or lost. If you're an outsider wanting to help, try directing the energies of children in more constructive ways - like supporting good parents. Encourage kids to obey. And insist on getting rid of laws that only serve to intimidate and isolate good parents.

My son, the youth minister in Ohio, called to tell me how successful his teenage summer retreat had been. I scowled as he joyously described a food fight between two hundred kids; if he'd thrown food around with the minister when he was a teenager, I'd have switched to a different religion. And I told him so. Rick had all the usual arguments down pat - "Everybody does it now" and "If we don't let them do their thing, we'll lose these kids."

Well, I've never known sensible behavior to lose a kid yet. And what about wasting all that food, when so many are homeless and starving? The next time you feel led to help the needy, let your kids hand-deliver the goods. It will keep them busy, and teach them a more valuable lesson than throwing food will. Some churches today must have more money than brains, and I'm going to remember that the next time they pass the collection plate.

And speaking of "more money than brains," remember - just as government creates or exaggerates problems when it wants to raise taxes, psychologists invent new trends to sell ideas, counseling sessions, books and programs. And organizations use them to attract the crowds and offerings they need. Weigh the motives before you buy their propaganda. Even if manners are old-fashioned, kids have to be taught not to make messes. And very few can afford to waste.

For some time now, society has been failing our kids - showing and telling them that self indulgence is better than law and order, that disrespect for others is a right of passage, and that irresponsibility and waste bring more pleasure than hard work. Morals are so old fashioned that children wallow in nudity, sex, and violence. Drug-related diseases and addictions are spreading like wildfire. And a million more high school girls have abortions each year.

For the sake of our children, we must get our act together. Reach out to your family members, your neighbors, and your friends. If fences need mending, go mend them. If you've withdrawn, branch out and get involved. If you care, act like it. If you've got helpful advice, speak up. And if things are less than perfect in your life, learn to listen.

My husband and I drove off to church last Easter Sunday morning, in our shiny new Town Car. The church was full of song and praise. Young families, with children dressed to please the Lord, filled the pews. And we (he claims my kids as his own) thought of our three kids in different states. We gave thanks that they'd all grown up okay, in spite of our mistakes. We prayed that God would bless every parent and guide every child, the way he had us. And we vowed to help, by sharing the things we learned while raising our kids.

Just as hickory sticks and leather straps from the good old days must remain a thing of the past, some of this new promiscuity must also go. Children still need a sensible code of conduct, rooted in good basic values, and enough firm but fair discipline to inspire them to follow it. Your kids need to be secure in your love. And that security comes from knowing you care enough to see that they get the things they need, that you have the strength to teach them to be honest and compassionate, and to take responsibility for their own actions, that you have the wisdom to guide them past activities with serious negative consequences, and to teach them to make decisions that will sustain and enhance their lives.

Parents must find a better way to insist that their small children obey immediately - the first time they're told. Time-out isn't working. No matter how smart your two-year old is, he doesn't comprehend that a speeding car will crush him, no matter how many times you tell him so. And when he's running toward the street as fast as his little legs can carry him, you may not have time to explain why he shouldn't go. You may not be close, or fast enough to restrain him. Would you rather he learn from the sting of your hand on his rear a few times, or would you prefer that the weight of steel and rubber all over his little body teach him respect for your word?

Did I say time-out wasn't working? That's because you spend more time ordering your two-year-old to stay on the chair than you spend explaining what he did wrong in the first place. By the time you repeat, "Get in time out" ten times, he's forgotten what he did to deserve it. His attention span is real short. And while you're screaming to override his protests, remember - he cannot yet comprehend what it's taken you twenty-five years to learn, even if he can pronounce the words. Try marching him to the chair immediately. Don't yell, 'cause he'll just learn to tune you out, long before you wear out. And you will wear out, long before yelling gets your message across. You don't have to shake him, or yank his little arm. And you don't have to hit him with an object that could injure him for life. Talk softly, and give him a big hand -lightly on the bare bottom with your finger tips. Sure the spanking will hurt a bit - probably you more than him. But it will make him think that facing you is too dastardly to risk further straying. If you're consistently persistent, the little guy will soon learn to stop the moment you say "no." And there may come a time when his life will depend on it.

Little things leave lasting impressions on children. A child dashed in front of me at the supermarket yesterday, and I nearly hit her with my cart. Her mother was too preoccupied with shopping to see the whole incident, but assumed it was my fault. "People just run you down for fun anymore," she said to her child, giving me an immediate look of contempt and disgust before moving on. I shook my head and walked away - a little embarrassed. Did she really think I would deliberately run down a child? I should have taken a minute to explain how lucky she was. If I'd been as vicious as she thought, or even as indifferent, the child would have probably been hit. If I'd been as rude as the mother, I'd have stayed for at least a shouting match. And worse yet, if I'd been a pervert, the child would have been in the back seat of my car.

I'm none of the above, and none of those things happened. But that mother sent her child some strong wrong messages - like "Most people don't care about you" and "it's easier to blame somebody else than to take responsibility for your actions." An apology to me wasn't necessary. I know kids get excited, and don't watch where they're going sometimes. But that little incident could have been used to give the child some new perspectives - like mistakes are okay, and people can be understanding when you stop to make things right.

Because our actions usually produce some kind of

reaction, children must be taught the "cause and effect" theory, at an early age. When we spare our kids the labor pains of learning, we deny them the pleasures of knowledgeable success. Remember how tough it was to spend your evenings studying, and how you hated those who made you do it? But wasn't it worth it when you stood at the head of the class with a 4.0 average, and then graduated to the highest-paying job in your chosen field? Unfortunately, in this less-than-perfect world, there are times when choosing between the lesser of two evils isn't quite as simple as studying harder for the "A" or playing video games and settling for a "D." Many times the reward for trying is less than an "A" but if we don't strive for it the world's mark will etch much deeper than the "D."

Today children witness too much glamour and ease, without realizing the negative side affects, until it's too late. If they're lucky, they just miss out on the feelings of achievement and the rewards of due diligence. If unlucky, they learn some mighty tough lessons the hard way. One thing's for sure - if you don't get through loud and clear to your children, somebody or something else will.

Not dealing with misdemeanors today may mean your child will have to face felonies tomorrow. When I was a kid, I stole a candy bar from the snack bar at school, where I was entrusted to work. Although confessing to the school secretary was painfully embarrassing, and losing my little job was costly, I still hadn't learned my lesson. Later I took a deck of cards from my aunt's house. Marching them back, with Mom and an open apology, was again humiliating - so humiliating that I finally realized "Crime does not pay." Both those experiences made me feel awful, and left me with permanent emotional scars - the kind that keep me from stealing to this very day.

A friend of mine also had sticky fingers. But his story is short. Rather than embarrass or humiliate her son, his mother ignored his petty little thefts. He was killed, in the process of committing armed robbery, some years later. Because he was deprived of the negative emotions that forbade crime, this child was void of an inner guidance counselor. If kids never learn that the stove is hot, chances are they'll get burned.

If they never have to wait for a moment's pleasure, they will never know the joy of anticipation, nor the elation of successful endurance. If they never shoulder a burden, they will never be able to carry their own weight. On the other hand, if they work to no avail, wait endlessly without reward, and carry your load, they will succumb to a world of defeat.

Balance discipline and training with love and fairness, and the kids will come to trust your judgement and learn to be just as fair. Get to the bottom of problems before placing blame. Defend your kids as adamantly when they are right, as you admonish them when they're wrong, and they will know you care. And don't forget to give them lots of love in between scoldings.

No matter how much money you have, don't spoil your child's ability to appreciate earning good things. If kids never have to earn anything, they never learn to make their own way. By two or three, they can start picking up their own stuff. Make sure they do a good job. By four they can start helping with small household chores. And by school age they can be doing enough to earn a little spending money. But don't pay them for everything. We all have to clean up our own messes, and contribute something where we live. Gradually add responsibilities. And don't forget to teach them to share and save. Mine used to have to give one dime from every dollar to church, or buy ice cream for a truly needy friend. They had to save a quarter from every dollar for at least six months, or until they had enough to buy something really special.

When our kids reach around the age of four or five, we parents start to get a break. Instead of doing a lot for them we get to do a lot with them. As they get older, reasoning takes center stage. Time-outs, deprivation, and grounding usually works if we take the time to explain why they're being corrected. And if not, a little humiliation and restitution will get the point across. Use everyday-life experiences to teach them. Share the telephone line and insist that they do the same. If they want a pet, see that they take care of it. If they're not getting good grades, ground them until they do. In your house, you make the rules. Kids will be free to meet the responsibilities of controlling their own houses soon enough. And right now you are helping to lay that foundation.

It's amazing - what a little truth, human understanding and good communication can bring. Talk with your kids, interact with them, and respect them. Make them respect you, and treat others accordingly. Never say no or make a promise, unless you mean it. We all have to keep our word. And remember - the objective is not to punish, nor to make your life easier. It is to keep your child safe and out of trouble while he or she prepares for adulthood. He or she must grow wise enough to make the choices that will enhance the rest of his or her life. And you have to do the teaching and listening.

Your kids will always have places to go, things to do, and friends to invite over. Encourage that all you can - after their responsibilities are met, of course. And although they need increasing freedom as they mature, don't forget to chaperon. Don't ever trust them enough to ignore your gut instincts. When the little voice inside says "I need to find out who that kid is with or what that kid is doing," heed it. It's your responsibility to see that they choose the right friends and engage in the right activities. Nothing will get a kid into trouble faster than hanging with the wrong crowd, going to the wrong places, and doing the wrong things - except maybe having nothing to do, and no parental supervision under which to do it. You must keep an eye on them.

By the time your kids are teenagers, you'll be fueling yourself with high octane. If you've taught them that cars crash, they'll probably drive themselves everywhere safely. If they don't, take the car. Insist on family cooperation from them, and see that they take responsibility for a large portion of their own care. If they don't, withdraw all the extras until they do. Reason with them as much as possible. But if they head down the path toward disaster, sit on them as long as you can. And when adulthood tugs unrelinquishingly at their hearts, hope and pray that they respect your word enough to discuss how to go the right way - before they make the break.

Instead of relying on government, take some affirmative action of your own. Find a balanced discipline that makes sense for you and your kids, and then stand up for it before all of society. Unite within your family and throughout your communities against government control and social decay. Join with other parents, and demand in unison that America be restored to the free and decent nation it once was. Empower your children and grandchildren to continue the tradition, so that all will remain safe and free.

And parents - don't forget to give yourself a break. Forgive your own mistakes, and recharge your batteries. You have rights too.

Take Back Control Of Your Schools

A friend complained that there was some controversy over whether her child was misbehaving in school or the teacher was being unfair (probably a little of both.) I suggested that she slip into the back of the classroom to observe occasionally. "Oh, I can't do that; the hallways are gated with steel mesh and outsiders need an escort. They have to be announced before entering a classroom," she said. "You're not an outsider, you're his mother," I argued. "Well they don't know that," she replied, "and besides, even parents can't be trusted these days."

You have got to be kidding! I hate sounding so critical, but the odds of having a child who doesn't need a parent to be involved in his or her learning process is about a trillion to one. So if the principal and teacher where your child goes to school don't know you're the parent, you had better get over there. If the teacher can't remember you any better than that, you should be down at the school board, fighting to get him or her fired. If your school is too big, or too far from home for you to get acquainted, you'd better be working with your community to build a more localized educational facility. And if you aren't showing your face enough, you aren't doing your job.

When you are denied access to your child, you are denied the opportunity to see that his or her needs are being met. And if you are not the first in line to see that your child is disciplined properly, your child may not behave well enough to learn in the classroom, and neither will the other students nearby. If you are not there to insist that your child be treated fairly, he or she probably won't be. If you do not see that the instructors you employ are doing a good job, they may not.

It's time to buck the system that no longer trusts or respects you as parents. And it's time to clean up the society that is forced to barricade parents in order to protect kids.

The government would have us believe that locking children in, and restricting access, is a necessary protective measure. But the more gates they install, the more violence runs rampant - both inside and out of our schools. Studies show that without strict parental supervision, the learning environment deteriorates, and that without parental participation in education, scholastic scores go down. Statistics also reveal that, for as long as the government has been shutting out parents, the greatest nation on earth has been falling behind much of the world academically, and morally.

I don't care how old-fashioned it sounds - steel gates and strangers acting as supervisors will never care and look after your kids the way you do. Besides, if there are that many criminals and perverts in America, who's to say some of them are not teachers, principals, janitors, and cooks. In fact, since children are most vulnerable, and predators dwell where there's plenty of prey, these perverts probably concentrate on landing jobs in our schools and day-care centers.

Perhaps it's time we brought parents back to replace the gates at school. Perhaps we should even arm them again. Sure somebody might get hurt, but it won't be the innocent kids all over this country. If perverts had to face parents who were free to protect their young, I bet they'd start playing with themselves instead of with our kids. We may never eliminate these deviates from society, but we can put them back in the closet where they belong.

Back in the sixties, instead of equally good schools and books for this nation's children, the government gave us bussing. And our children learned to live with its hardships. Under more powerful federal laws, rising costs of transportation, and an even heavier tax load, ordinary mothers of every race went to work to pay for it all. The government's legal maneuvering, and the economic restraints of sending children so far away from home for schooling, seriously impeded interaction between kids and parents. And the National Education Association had to take charge of our local schools.

When that proved to be so lucrative for government, they embarked on additional affirmative action programs designed to increase their money and power base. The profoundly handicapped and others too emotionally and/ or physically disturbed to learn to read and write were enrolled in mainstream public schools. And since freeing the parents of America's disadvantaged children to work generated more tax dollars and control than academic achievement did, the government started holding back super kids. Programs designed to keep over-achievers satisfied where they were, instead of moving those capable of advancing up and out, was added to the curriculum. Before long the NEA had turned our schools into baby sitting and special privilege facilities, while the vast majority of American children got left out in the cold academically, morally, and emotionally. And we've been sliding down hill ever since.

With public schools in the firm grip of the Feds, poverty, crime, and ignorance increased without racial boundaries, in the ghetto and throughout the countryside. As the crime rate soared, the NEA started locking kids in and restricting parental access - as a necessary protective measure of course. But the more gates they installed, the more violence we saw. And without strict parental supervision and participation in education, the learning environment deteriorated. Scholastic scores went down even further.

After a while, American parents of every race and class which had been previously designated by the government started demanding better results in unison. Government leaders groped for ways to stay in control, and as a result - affirmative action based on "family status" was born. Refer to chapter five for more details. Once again, government leaders used our concerns as an excuse to tax and regulate instead of solving our problems. Once Again, they concentrated attention on moving our children instead of addressing the real educational needs. Only this time, instead of mandating bussing they provided incentives that would inspire parents to move, they infringed on private property rights, and they violated a lot of other rights in the process. Businesses were forced to give parents incentives to keep working, certain advertising was banned, and another wedge of division separated America's young families from supposedly older better-established citizens.

With real family values out the window, and government's interpretation in, child-related violence increased. And the government had another excuse to take more affirmative action - preschool to relieve working parents and overburdened grandparents, and the implementation of a child's right to sue in court. Under the protection of these new laws, four-year-olds began attending public schools, kids started filing law suits against moms and dads with the government's blessing, and children started murdering their parents. God forbid over-zealous parents speak out - lest they be accused of denying children their rights.

What's the next step - programming kids to shoot their parents for the sake of the state? Before you label me a radical, I beg you to review the history leading up to World War II, and compare it to the state of affairs in the U.S. right now. With so many freedoms down the tubes, and Americans required to document every move, think about it - the only thing our federal government lacks today, that Nazi Germany had yesterday, is an army of youth, willing to bear arms against their own friends, neighbors, and families. And they're working on that.

Enter Mr. and Mrs President Clinton - asking Congress to bust down your door without knocking to search for drugs, asking for higher academically accounting to the federal government instead of better grades, classrooms divided in half instead of an agenda that would enable group interaction, government baby sitting before and after class instead of parental guidance and supervision, mandatory summer school instead of parks and playgrounds, and uniforms for American's school kids.

HELLO AGAIN. Call it what you will, but leaving the majority of our children at school from daylight till dark and all summer long is not education - its "institutionalizing." Right down to the uniform dress code, we are starting to look more like Nazi Germany and Red China every day.

I know several people who like the idea of school uniforms. I've heard everything from "Uniforms keep the focus off cloths and on school work" to "Uniforms eliminate peer pressure." All I can say is "Review your history books." Medicine mandated by the government is usually a pretty bitter pill to swallow, and it's almost always given to the wrong citizen for the wrong illness.

The Clintons say they never want you to choose between the job you need and the child you love again. So they propose that the state raise your taxes and your children, and that your employer give you time off work when it's necessary to visit your kids or take them to the doctor. Get real. It's no coincidence that just when many parents are thinking about adjusting to one taxable income for the sake of their kids, these leaders come up with the rhetoric that will make staying at work seem easier and more profitable than being at home.

The government's agenda is "number present and under control," not freedom, safety or relevant educational needs met. Naturally, the Clintons think less child care worries and a higher minimum wage are good. The more Americans they keep working, and the more those citizens make, the more tax dollars the government collects. And now they have nowhere to turn for a larger enrollment except toward mainstream American kids. This government is about money and power, not the welfare of our kids. And once the rules are in place, and the money to enforce them is deducted from your paycheck, you don't have to like the results.

Speaking of results - where are we going to find enough qualified teachers to do the job? Under the direction of the

NEA, the atmosphere in public schools has become so intolerable that many of our best teachers are switching to different careers. They are forced to provide sex education to kids unable to read and write. They hand out condoms and birth control pills to prevent pregnancy and AIDS, but can't give an aspirin to a child with a headache. And in many schools, their very lives are on the line.

Where are they going to find the space and funding? Schools are already over-crowded and under-funded everywhere. The one hundred thousand new teachers and five thousand new schools the President has room for in his budget isn't enough to divide the classrooms in Florida, let alone handle the load of latch-key kids all over this country. In fact, many schools have recently cut seventh period because they can't afford to keep kids all day. Never mind that it's too long a day for the very young and the severely handicapped.

So is President Clinton proposing another plan to send the nation's children farther down the slide? Of course he is. He doesn't care whether the program works, or whether it's good for our kids. Bill is in the dog house right now. And Hillary's new cause is the quickest and easiest way out. It touches her heart, as well as ours.

Just remember - the only things the Clintons are pro-choice on are abortion, free and easy sex any way they can get it, the right of children to sue their parents, and the global economic advancement of foreign dictators. Under the leadership of this President, the government fed our kids poison Mexican strawberries for lunch, and the NEA rewrote American history books to depict our Revolutionary War heroes as the bad guys. This President believes in bussing our kids as far away from home as possible. He enhances Chinese nuclear capabilities, and fills our hope chests with Chinese products.

And don't forget, this administration was elected under the shadow of suspicion - swindling money from their favorite political party, selling out to foreign enemies, the illegal use of public funds, sexually harassing young women who work in our stately offices, and maybe even murder.

This President embarrassed his own daughter by cheating on his wife for fun. He humiliated the Lewinskys by taking head from Monica under the Oval Office desk. His denials have already cost the American taxpayer over forty million dollars. And we don't even know about the string of dead bodies left in his wake yet. What if he's lying about them too? Would this Presidential couple kill, and cover it up? I don't know. But is risking the future of our children to another admitted pervert, and the good judgement of a wife who supports him, worth taking a chance on? I think not.

But you're going let them dress your kids, and baby sit your children after school? What's wrong with you? Are you crazy, or do you find it easier to go to work and support the government than to nurture your own young? Why else would you entrust the well-being of your kids to a couple who would blur the off-color stories linking them to murder and sexual assault by focusing in on the nation's children? And why else would you trust an institution with the National Educational Association's miserable track record of failure to raise your kids?

Come home Mom or Dad. Your schoolhouse is on fire, and your children will burn. Again - statistics clearly show that the moral, emotional, and academic standings of our children have been declining drastically ever since the government took control of our schools. Under the direction of the NEA, our kids are falling behind the rest of the world in all three categories. Healthy American children are being forced to attend class with known HIV carriers. And the majority of our kids are going without the educational tools necessary to help them achieve. Violence runs rampant inside and out of our schools. Parents have been degraded, regulated, and taxed into staying away. Many of our best teachers are leaving the public school system. While society is out protecting animals, kids are threatening them with guns and knives. For fear of being falsely accused, killed, sued, or misjudged, caring instructors and parents refuse to reach out to kids, or to correct them with love. The needs of under-and-over achievers have taken priority over profoundly-average academics, even though most of

America's students are average. Discipline has succumbed to bureaucratic nonsense. And protection from disease and physical harm are reserved for no one.

The government is selling you a bill of no-goods. You're buying a product that doesn't work, from a company that can't deliver the quality your children deserve. Excuse me, but the whole stinking system sucks. And it's costing Americans more than they can afford. In fact, it's become so unaffordable that we legalized government gambling to ease the financial load. Remember when lotteries were banned because they were bad? Now those profiteering enterprises are just off-limits to ordinary free-enterprising Americans, because only gangsters and governments are wise enough to handle that much evil. Education only gets twenty cents out of every dirty dollar, and administrative costs are eating up the other eighty, because they're dealing off the bottom - to themselves. Didn't anybody ever tell you that when it takes more to get to work than it does to do the job, it's time to quit.

Contrary to the latest propaganda, the resources of the fittest are limited. And lest they run out, we'd better start using them more wisely. How 'bout a little citizen common sense here too? We can help each child in this country, from the least capable to the most advanced, reach his or her full potential, without sacrificing anyone - just by taking back control of our educational system, cleaning up our schools, and returning them to the learning centers they once were.

We must demand that the government return our kids to neighborhood schools, and restore local control. Once we're back in charge of the educational future of our children, we can start recognizing each set of individual needs, and accommodating them accordingly - for real. Every community has the resources to safely and adequately care for and school all their children - simply by redistributing the wealth away from federal and state governments, and back to where it belongs - in the hands of good and sensible people. Right now administrative costs are consuming eighty cents out of every dollar we pay for education. And even our lending institutions know that an

80/20 split won't work, unless it's in favor of the family and local community.

So let's reverse the government's greedy trend. For that twenty percent we now get, federal and state agencies can develop all the academic standards and guidelines necessary to keep us on an even keel. And with the eighty percent they're getting, we can more than implement those standards. So why not do the switch? Tell government leaders to form a committee from among the ranks of their idle and get cracking on it. And if you think we aren't paying for a lot of idleness, check out all the empty congressional seats on the C-span channel. Maybe we should demote some of them back to the local level. With eighty percent of their funds and more responsibility for education shifted to the local level, there will be a lot of academic work to do back home.

Granted, we need to enhance school curriculums. But learning to feed and toilet oneself is not part of the agenda for higher learning - and neither is it called for. Believe it or not, most parents know that infants need more basic care than any institutional learning center can provide. And they are still teaching their kids to master these basic life functions before sending them to school. Because there are a few kids who don't have families to nurture them, we will have to make sure we have some good children's homes, and special care facilities. But housing and basic care will fall under another department. Don't worry - when government waste is a thing of the past, plenty of funds will be available to meet those needs.

As for before-and-after school child care - if there is a real demand, our free enterprise system will find a way to provide the service at affordable prices. And uniforms - well I don't think our government has been indoctrinating these kids long enough to get away with telling them what to wear. Besides, American parents can still afford to put shirts on the backs of their kids, and can still keep the dress code under control if they try. Kids may not all look alike, or feel the same. But the right to be different is what freedom's all about.

Ten percent of our educational dollars should be dedicated to the academic enhancement of those who are permanently disabled or long-term ill. Although their numbers are few, and equipment to accommodate them is somewhat expensive; we must provide them the opportunity to reach their full potential.

And we'll have to be more sensible about quarantining kids with contagious diseases, including AIDS. If we expect to excel, we must not allow contagions to be spread to our healthy, nor our institutions of higher learning turned into infirmaries for the sick. And we do expect to excel, don't we?

As for our geniuses between the ages of five and eighteen - move them up, just like we used to. If your ten-year-old can function on the college level, don't hold him back. Get him a computer, and send him off to Yale. There's plenty of scholarship money available. And if he's that smart, he's going to advance somewhere - better in an institute of higher learning, than in the custody of Uncle Sam, or on the streets today. Here again, government needs millions, because parents and schools supposedly can't handle the emotional needs of their gifted children. You're worried about exposing these kids to adult activities before they're ready to cope? Come now - even the average achiever can pack a gun, purchase drugs from the street corner pharmacy, and practice safe sex in fifth grade. That's more grown up than we are. Besides, ten per cent of the budget is more than adequate. As you can see from the grade reports coming out of schools today, over-achievers are few and far between. And since they invent as they go, they need little help breezing through school.

If we are to survive as a free species of human beings, we must maintain a facility geared toward the acceleration of America's mainstream kids. They are the majority - and it takes a majority of able bodies and minds to keep any nation free and prosperous enough to take care of themselves, as well as their weak. Forty cents out of every educational dollar will do. That's twice as much as the government gives us. And statistics show that even in the poorest ghettos, we can bring kids up to par academically on one-eighth of what the government needs - especially if the folks in those communities are as anxious to pitch in as they say they are.

We have practical designs for modern learning centers, and local construction crews in every part of the country, willing to build and remodel for reasonable fees. But we won't need as many small classrooms as you think. I've looked at mainstream text books, and examined the curriculums. The books are filled with neat things we never dreamed of learning. The agenda includes real-life experiments that provide our kids opportunities to reach out into fields we've never begun to explore. With that much to occupy their minds, thirty normal, well-behaved kids can easily learn together - especially when they know why they are there, and what's expected of them.

Good physical and mental health must be the prerequisites for getting in. Children must be capable of functioning academically before entering, or we defeat the purpose of education before we even begin. The good old-fashioned kindergarten level seems like the appropriate place to start. Granted, the average kid today can already count a little, knows the alphabet and primary colors, and understands more about safety rules than we ever did. They have all the basic functions (like eating and going to the bathroom) down pat. And they are emotionally more mature at an earlier age than we were. But they can use that extra year in kindergarten to adjust their behavior from play to the learning mode. And their social skills need some fine tuning. Aren't all these positive changes exciting?

And speaking of behavior - they say our society is decaying because our children are no longer being taught to make moral decisions. I know we must be careful to keep church and state separate, and that Americans believe too differently to find a national religious compromise. But if we don't start deciding what's right and wrong for ourselves, the government is going to do it for us. Right now, while we're all so busy trying to avoid stepping on our neighbor's spiritual toes, the government is writing an encyclopedia on how to restore law and order. Its founded on principles from somebody's Bible. And if we don't stop the looting and pilfering and murder among our youth, they're going to print it in large bold enforceable letters. Let's police our own kids, so the government will have no excuse to.

Religious teachings are missing from the present educational agenda, and that is as it should be. But maybe, just to keep our society from turning into a wild-life preserve, we should revise school handbooks to include a new chapter called "Social Law and Order." Maybe the table of contents should go something like this: honor thy father and mother, no dirty language, thou shalt not assault or kill, thou shalt not become intoxicated on drugs or booze, thou shalt not steal, lie, nor cheat, and thou shalt respect the rights of others as thou expects to be respected. Reenforcing that simple code of ethics at home, at school, and throughout the streets where children roam, should be mandatory homework for every American. How else can we explain that slaying the neighbor, and snatching his coke will lead to nothing but trouble?

We allow our little ones to play with adult toys, like money and sex and guns, too soon. And we spare them the consequences too long. So naturally, we see more kids murdering, buying drugs, and having sex too young. Too many children are venturing into these areas before they understand the negative repercussions, or know how to cope with them responsibly. And they're getting hurt. How 'bout some instruction to go with that "Social Law and Order" handbook - a class to explain the consequences of social disorder, and some new lesson plans that teach children how to behave in a civilized society?

When my mother thought it was about time for me to start my period, she gave me a book on the birds and the bees. Of course I could read. But I was more interested in flying with birds than in learning about where they came from. Reassured that I had given that boring book enough attention, and that I knew better than to take my pants off, Mom went on with a more comfortable agenda. And when I got pregnant, about three years later, we were both surprised - she being sure I knew better, and me wondering how it happened, and what the consequences were going to be. Now supposedly we've come a long way, Baby. But you can't prove it by the number of young unwed mothers still dropping out of high school today.

Obviously, we still don't have enough right answers to keep our kids from getting in over their heads too young. We need to reevaluate ineffective sex and drug education. The NEA approach isn't working, and psychology books to date have only made things worse. Even Drug Abuse Resistance Education (DARE) admits that their success is not lasting. Part of the problem may be timing -starting too soon, waiting too long, failing to notice the signs of the time when we should. I don't have all the answers either. But we must try something different. How 'bout some new research in these areas - the kind that analyzes real-life problems kids face, and gears some realistic feedback toward parental and community control? Some new lessons might help - the kind that include parental participation, leadership, and supervision instead of subsidized government control. And maybe we parents should go back to school for that class.

Maybe we should all be setting a better example? We build our homes in deed-restricted subdivisions because we don't want to live with offensive odors, obnoxious behavior, and distractive noises. Yet we fail to teach our children manners. We won't tolerate cursing from our neighbor's neatly-landscaped lawn, but our children go to school in ragged jeans and oversized T shirts sporting dirty words. We sunbathe behind privacy-fenced pools while our children watch everything from nude perfume commercials to rape to seven acts of sexual intercourse a day. And we debate fit punishment for murderers while our children watch eighteen thousand violent crimes a year on television.

The media would have us believe that the birth control pills of today make better chaperons than old-fashioned parents ever did. Well, maybe it's time we parents helped the media clean up their act, too. Once we turn off the trash in our family rooms, and refuse to buy the products supporting it, their gross revenues will drop, along with the nasty shows. Now that's setting our kids free to get on with their studies.

Freedom - kids won't understand that term until we start teaching its meaning. While we've been busy, shuffling them back and forth between two jobs, the government has been disguising freedom as assistance, and then trading it off. But with every swap, Americans lose more than they gain. The definition is already gone from our history books. And at the current rate of exchange, any bargaining chips that might bring it back will be long spent by the time today's little guys reach school age. We must do something to reverse this trend. Along with more reading, writing, and arithmetic, how 'bout reinstating an old-fashioned American History course in school, and some accelerated insight related to the dangers of government control by appeasement?

Militia groups are springing up all over the country. And their youthful members are being portrayed as radical, insane, and criminal - just like Nathan Hale. But these young people are our ignorant children - the ones we failed to teach that the Revolutionary and Civil Wars were already fought and won by Americans. When was the last time you reached out to a militant teenager, and showed him or her that our founding fathers gave us the power to preserve freedom and bring change without assassinating each other with guns and bombs? When was the last time you showed a young person how freedom really works?

Since actions speak louder than words, let's show them that their forefathers left us a better, more peaceful way to bring change. Let's restore their power to quietly think for themselves, and their freedom to speak up when it counts. Let's show them that the prosperity of a free enterprise system and the right to vote is still alive - and able to work in America today. Instead of writing them off, let's show our dissident kids how to contact their congressman, and get good results.

It's time for an All-American tax cut - twenty percent in this one department alone. It's cheaper to buy education for children than it is to support Uncle Sam. And you deserve to keep more of what you earn. Besides, a twenty percent tax savings on two incomes will enable a lot of parents to stay home. And just think of all the family enhancements that'll buy - no child care fees; transportation and clothing costs greatly reduced; the elimination of an unhealthy fast food diet, not to mention the expense; time to clip coupons and invest the savings in the stock market; and less stress-related medical bills. Think of all the heartaches families can avoid by taking care of their kids, and all the loving fun that will come from someone being at home for them. Take my word for it - all the precious memories made at home beats reminiscing about office strife when you're old and gray.

Let's show our children what the majority in a free country can really achieve - perpetual competitive excellence for all.

Call Out The Press

When the government shut down for lack of budgeted funding back during Clinton's first term, one reporter, in one brief CNN report, mentioned that our national parks had been closed. He said park rangers had been furloughed, campers and hikers had been ejected, armed guards were stationed at park entrances, and steel barricades were being erected to keep citizens out - all for the good public's safety.

I flew into a rage and gasped, "To keep us safe from what?" We tamed the Wild West, and walked on the moon. We sail the seven seas, and pound the pavement in New York City. We bungi jump, ski dive, scale mountains, and drive the Los Angeles freeways. I reckon we can traipse across Yellowstone without a government chaperon. And even if we can't, we still have the right to try.

Haunted by the reflection of my Father's image in the mirror, I tried to get a grip on myself. But I had too many questions. How could a "shut down" government bar anyone from anything, anywhere? If the government couldn't afford to pay our rangers, how could they afford armed guards to evict us, and contractors to build and install steel barricades to keep us off the land we bought and paid for with our tax dollars? And since when does a government of and for and by the people hire armed guards to evict, and erect steel barricades to bar free people from their property? How can elected representatives in a free country remain functional enough to control us, but not functional enough to provide the services we employ them to perform?

Besides, how'd they get steal barricades built so fast, and contractors all the way out there to install them immediately upon shutdown? Could confiscation of the peoples' land have been the first planned move of an officially shut-down-government? That's scary!

I stayed glued to the television, waiting to hear my questions answered. I switched channels, and sat through hours of repetitious interviews, repetitive debates, and speculation as to which political party was to blame for the budget crunch, but never once heard the barricades mentioned again. My questions were never even raised, let alone answered. During all those weeks of speculative budget debate, the media never once asked how a government, too poor to provide its citizens service, afforded to control the land of the free.

Nobody seemed to realize that having our public property confiscated by the government was a serious threat to freedom. And the press was doing nothing to arouse public awareness. If the media had substituted just one political personality comparison for some examples of people living in countries where the government has the power to confiscate property, more of us might have paid attention. Remember those displaced families in Bosnia - mothers dragging their hungry kids through miles of mud, with every possession they owned riding on their backs? If the media had sacrificed just one talk show for some shots of our shut-down government, busily barricading our national parks with foreign-made steel, maybe we'd have realized that our government was just as capable of closing up front and running out the back with our assets as any foreign dictator is. If the media had answered some of my questions and stayed on that story, like they did on the President's sex life, more of you might have finally realized just how close to unfree we really are.

But let's be fair. Although the media didn't answer all my questions, they provided enough information to sound an alarm. I just didn't respond. I wrote some editorials, but never sent them in. I tried to call Rush Limbaugh a few times, but didn't stay tuned long enough to get through. I tried to involve my friends, but they thought I misunderstood the report. Naturally, as I cooled off, the urgency to protest waned. And my notes on the dangers of government barricades went into the dead file, along with all the other abuses of their power we've failed to check.

Granted, the free press that used to be the unrelenting voice of liberty and the watch dog of freedom has not been keeping us well informed lately. But then we haven't exactly been jumping out of bed to act when they bark an alarm either. In spite of all our faults, free citizens and the free press need each other. As much as the media depends upon an audience to buy their product, liberty demands that self-governing citizens be armed with the truth. And we all depend on freedom of speech. It's time to lick our wounds, and come together for the cause.

The press is trying. When that couple illegally captured Newt Gingrich on tape, and flaunted his conversation in front of the media, I felt so sorry for reporters - so embarrassed for them. It was so obvious that they were being used. And that made them mad enough to start changing the program in spite of our lack of support. Within a month, we saw a new cable channel challenge government activities. "The Fleecing of America" on NBC nightly news, and other spotty programs with a hint of discontent began to air.

Are you watching those shows, and responding favorably? Are you providing the commentators feedback, and buying the products of advertisers who support freedom? Are you scolding your congressman when he fleeces America, and boycotting the companies who participate with him?

The men and women of the press don't like being the government's mouthpiece - spreading confusion, fear, and socialism. But what choice do they have? They have to respond to the cries they hear. And they hear screaming and crying for government aid, protection, and intervention - not self-sufficient people shouting, "give me liberty or give me death."

Reporters have been warning us and asking freedom-loving Americans to support them for years. They warned of back-stabbing government secrecy when leaders used cold-war antics as an excuse to operate undercover and the Kennedy assassinations to justify securing public figures behind closed doors. But for fear our national defenses would be compromised and our public servants slain in the streets, we the people forfeited our right to an open honest government - and left our most respected commentators scrounging outside for factual information.

When government leaders offered appeasement in the form of regimented press conferences, we bought it. Right now, good reporters stoop to unscrupulous tactics, just trying to get at unattainable truths, while we pick up the tab for government's expensive professional speech writers and spokespersons - all because our top leaders (most of whom have graduated from renounced universities) aren't articulate enough to speak for themselves. And we're still subsidizing college educations and scheduled press conferences. We're getting just what we pay for: well-written and rehearsed evasions instead of truth, cream puff orations and misleading tidbits instead of the facts - all designed to make us surmise what leaders want us to think, and all leaked when they want us to think it.

Our press complains bitterly, but we leave them hanging right between scandalous leaders who didn't want to be exposed, and a bunch of socialists screaming for a free ride from Uncle Sam.

No wonder our free press is confused - and confused they are. The press helps perpetuate those mixed musical messages that leave us confused about crime, the economy and our strength as a nation. They portray Castro as a humanitarian while our own citizens are still trying to free their loved ones from his brutal clutches. They support peaceful negotiations with terrorists - unless and until our Commander in Chief needs a bomb-shell victory overseas to get him off the sexual hot seat at home.

The media reflects on polls depicting Bill and Hillary Clinton, "the most admired couple in U.S. history," while the President lies under oath and the First Lady sets the movement to liberate women back twenty years. And as Mr. and Mrs. Clinton advocate free sex in the White House, we wonder what negative effects their example of sexual incompatibility and infidelity will have on American families.

The press sides with American leaders who position themselves for international power and wealth, without ever mentioning that the gluttons have to go global for power and money because they've already taken most of ours. Commentators advocate government care-taking, but their own statistics reflect the fact that most of the food and money we already entrust the government to deliver never actually reaches those desperate needy faces we see on television.

Most of us realize that both man and beast are safer and more prosperous in a democracy than in a government-controlled society. But there are still too many reporters around who believe the government should take care of us. They don't understand that when government gives, we ultimately pay too heavy a price. And we must help them see the light.

If my local bleeding heart liberal socialist reporter can be turned right, there's hope for the rest. My local guy thought government should change everything that inconvenienced him. He thought that, on top of saving more of the environment, government should halt local development so he wouldn't have to travel through construction zones. He thought the government should regulate "the Christmas thing" so he wouldn't have to contend with extra shoppers and long lines too early. And he relayed that information to the public by way of his newspaper editorials.

I couldn't stand to think that our free press was in the hands of someone so unable to see the value of freedom and prosperity, and so blind to the dangers of government control. So via a letter to the editor, I let him know that there were countries in the world that did control what their citizens bought, and when they bought it. But I suggested that he check out the selections on their shelves, before deciding to relocate to one of them. My mother scolded me for being so harsh, and we wrote a second letter - just to help him understand. Since I can find no better way to make my point, let me share that letter with you.

Dear Bill,
"Throughout the year, while you were thinking of ways for the government to solve your problems, we were learning to compromise, share, and live in harmony with all earth's creatures without giving up freedom. We were sponsoring research and education. We were teaching our children how to better utilize the natural resources being preserved for them, and how to prosper without destroying their environment. Throughout the year, while you were trying to convince us that the government should and could solve our problems, we were working, developing, and finding ways to solve our own. For every acre we used to create jobs and provide upscale housing for our ever-growing population, we preserved several acres for future generations. For every tree we cut to make room, we planted three. While you complained of too much commercialism, we prospered and gave of that prosperity. We supplied food, clothing, and even blood to millions destroyed by dictatorships around the world. At home, we set up shelters for the homeless and victims of disaster. And we provided welfare, food stamps, and medical care to millions more. While you were doing "the Christmas thing" we were celebrating the birth of Jesus Christ. For weeks before Christmas, we shopped, baked, and went to parties with friends. But not before we gave to those less fortunate, and not before we did our best to make sure every child had a new toy under the tree. On Christmas Eve, we went to church and prayed for the safe return of our young men and women keeping the peace around the world. We prayed for the suffering in Bosnia, Cuba, Red China, and other suppressed countries. And we gave thanks for the American jobs and freedom and prosperity that enables us to help them all. On Christmas Day, we made room at our tables for family we hadn't seen in months, cared for neighbors, reminisced with our elderly relatives, and gave gifts to our loved ones. Around a bountiful Christmas dinner, we taught our five-year old great granddaughter to help by setting the table. On

the day after Christmas, we had the opportunity to read your opinion. We prayed that God would give you the wisdom and strength to meet the responsibilities that go with your "free press" privileges. As another tree is cut to make the paper you write on, and readers pay for another subscription, we pray that you'll remember that millions have given their lives so that we could live in this free land of prosperity, and that you'll do your part to encourage and preserve that freedom. For the sake of your children and ours, we pray you'll see and print the truth.
(Ending salutations.)

Isn't it time you called your local reporters to the cause of freedom, and lined up behind them for the fight? You'll have to do more than watch and complain. In fact, we're all going to have to do more. Just as reporters must reorganize their thoughts and redirect their pens toward the unbiased unopinionated truth, we must support their efforts to get at that truth. And we must act when they sound the alarm.

Remember - this is not about left or right, conservative or liberal, Democrat or Republican, nor the people against the press. We're all citizens. This is about freedom and open honest government - something none of us have gotten from any of our elected officials, on either side of the fence, for far too long.

The next time your favorite reporter asks a question and gets hushed by the political spokesman - protest. Insist that your representative give honest, straightforward answers. Before long, only truthful candidates will be leaking the news. Back candidates who are clean enough to expose themselves, and their activities candidly to our free press; tune out those who do not, and transmit your demands for freedom to government representatives, through the channels of communication opened up by the media.

There are two things we can be sure of. One - when the media starts bombarding us with pictures and stories about peoples from a foreign dictatorship who are starving and being misused, we are being prepared to come to their aid, financially, militarily, or both. And two - when we start hearing reports about a hazardous material, dangerous activity, or problems that somebody wants solved here at home, more taxes and government controls are coming our way.

When we saw and heard a lot about Mexico and China, we got those new trade agreements. When we heard about the harmful agents of smoking, we practically got cigarettes banned. Recently we've been hearing a lot about flooding, and guess what - the government just launched a multi-billion dollar program to map American streams. And they're working on a multi-trillion dollar campaign to buy the property adjacent to them. So if you live in the thirty year flood plain, be prepared to move away from the government agency rushing to harness your water - or call out the press to turn the tide.

Right now we're hearing about skirmishes in several hot spots, and terrorist activities around the world. And heaven only knows how much campaign fund reform, sexual misconduct, bad business practices, and all the other unethical sins being broadcast from Washington will cost us. But you mark my words - the price will be high in dollars, lives, and liberties. How 'bout asking the press to start making the danger connection right up front, and hitting the cost as heavily as they lay on the sorrow, fear, and guilt?

We must make the media aware that the slant they give each story, coupled with the information they withhold, contributes greatly to our indoctrination. During the 1996 Presidential campaign, CNN followed Bob Dole around. They even filmed the moving and enthusiastic ninety-six-hour "Rock Around The Clock" side of his campaign. But we never saw it - except for one brief glimpse too late on election day to affect voters. It was a far cry from the constant pre-election showings of a frail Dole falling off that platform, followed by concerns that Boris Yeltsin's concealed weakened heart might not endure. If that's not deliberate subtle conditioning, I don't know what is.

When churches burned, media put the emphasis on "black" instead of catching the arsonist. Headlines reeled of multiracial clashes in cities like Los Angeles, between citizens, aliens, and police. But the way the press presented it, we couldn't tell the good guys from the bad in any of the categories. The news played up "black" and "white" juries handing down different O.J. Simpson verdicts, while an unidentified killer of whatever color went free. And every time we turn on the television, we hear another racial statistic, based on another opinion poll we were never called on to answer - still pitting black against white. Tell them it's time to change the color of their print - to beige.

My pet peeve is that we're bombarded with the same flashy snapshots, hours of repetitive rhetoric, debates and opinions on everything from "liberal versus conservative philosophy" to "who lies or who tells the truth" - while real events that seriously erode our freedoms barely get mentioned or go unnoticed. When Clinton was out taking credit for so many new business start-ups, even our own Rush Limbaugh showed the President over and over again at one funeral - switching from laughter to tears every time the camera focused on him. Limbaugh's attempts to convince us that the President wasn't on the level might have worked if he'd substituted just a few of those laugh-cry shots with some pictures of all the businesses that folded during Clinton's first term.

Hey, you media guys - how 'bout some variety here? When you find you're repeating yourself, why not slip in a little freedom propaganda every third hour or so.

And speaking of reminiscing - how 'bout replacing some of those old Nazi flicks with some footage from the archives of more recent American history. If the media could turn boring old budget talks into weeks of profitable air time, just think what they can do with steel barricades and armed guards ousting American citizens from their national parks. How 'bout going back eight years, and reviewing your old notes with a new attitude. Write some new stories, and show us some new clips of all the exciting things you skimmed over and left out. And instead of accenting the government's best side, try sensationalizing freedom.

If television can turn routine office activities at the White House and a kiss on the cheek from Monica Lewinsky into a national scandal, just think what they can do with the trail of accidental and coincidental deaths left behind the President. We love entertainment, but the news is serious business. Come on, you media guys - give us some facts to go with the fun.

While you're promoting all these new trade agreements, we're asking how many lives and how much money they will cost future Americans. While you claim we have a big budget surplus, we're trying to figure out how it got balanced overnight. While you speculate on how to spend the surplus, we worry about how to pay off the national debt. Tell the truth - is the budget balanced, or are we still trying to figure out how to pay off a two hundred billion dollar debt to the U.N.? And before the government shuts down again, tell us the whole story - which congressmen prefer holiday furloughs to doing their jobs? Which want to spend more billions than we can afford, and which ones are willing to shaft Americans in the process? How many freedoms will they take to do it?

Speaking of employees - how 'bout some news on the good guys. You rarely find me defending public officials these days. But besides the cost of advertising being too high for most Americans, few of us are perfect enough to endure the public scrutiny. So naturally the country is running short on good people who can afford to serve. By cutting us some slack in the personal areas, and giving the good guys some free exposure, the press can probably bring some very qualified public servants out of the woodwork.

Although polls may reveal that we don't care about the private sex lives of our leaders, we do need to know who's honest and obeying the law. And we need to know if they're doing a good job for us. Since we don't have time to watch CNN and CSPAN all day long, how 'bout challenging the media? All you local stations out there - assign a reporter to every local branch of government (city, county, regional, state.) Hey major networks - cover CSPAN, and all the feds. CNN - how 'bout a little freedom news, to go with your French fashion shows? Don't worry about nobody tuning in; millions of us listen to Rush Limbaugh, and even those who wish he'd go away can't tune him out - because the state of the nation weighs so heavy upon our hearts and minds these days.

Don't forget to seriously scrutinize every commission and department, at every level of government. Keep tabs on every piece of legislation, and sniff out all those little laws that whisk away our freedoms when nobody's paying attention. You won't have time to repeat each chapter and verse, or render an opinion on the air. But you could give viewers in your area an "alert summary" on the evening news. Just tell them things like how much got spent that day and on what, how many more acres of land the various branches of government bought, and how many new laws stole how many liberties that day. While you're at it, give us a head count - the number of public servants employed (both elected and appointed at every level of government) compared to the number absent each day.

Imagine reading the local newspaper, and hearing radio and television reporters question our elected officials directly about their response to the demands of American people! Imagine the excitement - when every newspaper and radio and television station is joined with us in support of the cause of freedom. And just imagine the response we'll get from freedom-loving people everywhere, when every station announces that we are no longer going to tolerate being regulated into extinction. Just imagine the strength and liberty of a people united behind the free press. It sure would be a pleasant change.

Reclaim Your Land

A customer glancing through my <u>Today's Realtor</u> noticed an article about property rights, and called me on the carpet for not saving his. He assured me that he wasn't a radical, but that he agreed with the Boston Tea Party, American women who won the right to vote by protesting, and colored Americans marching and winning freedom. And he praised realtors in Florida for uniting and bombarding Tallahassee until the state eliminated the service tax. "Yeah, we tied up their phone lines until they set us free," I boasted.

"Well, I wouldn't brag too loud if I were you," he said. "The National Association of Realtors (NAR) is the largest real estate organization in the world. They pay lobbyists from clear down here at the county seat all the way up to Washington. And they can't do nothing to stop the government from taking my land." This old man owned a large farm somewhere in the Mid West. But when the government refused to let him plat off a homestead for his youngest son, he got mad, sold the farm, and moved to Florida.

He asked if I knew how many regulations, limiting or taking away private property rights, had been passed during the last ten years. "Hundreds of thousands" I answered, but I couldn't give him the exact number. "That's because there's too many to count," he said. And after instructing me to find him a house without restrictions, he stomped out of my office.

My experience as a real estate professional has taught me one thing - that he who owns the land controls it and everything it's used for. Land is the foundation of our food, housing, and prosperity. Having our land bought up and our public property confiscated by the government is more than a serious threat to freedom - it's a threat to our very existence. And I'm here to tell you that I've been watching our private property rights disappear into the hands of the government for quite some time.

Homeowners along the coast must plow through pages of complicated regulations, pay a fee, and get a permit before they can trim the Mangrove trees in their back yards. My neighbor just paid a fine because he didn't know he had to have a permit to patch the tar on his shingled roof. I sympathized with a local Floridian who paid at least thirty thousand in engineering, attorney, and application fees just to find out he could not use one of his ten acres for a home site. And I anguished with a customer who had to give the government twenty acres, for the right to put a one-acre driveway up to his house.

I know of numerous owners who've sold out to the government in the last few years, and I wonder where they've gone. One man was in a particular bind. Because they found a Scrub Jay nest on his land, government agents refused to let him divide it into building lots for home sites. Yet they continued to assess it for taxes as if it had useable value - to the tune of four thousand a year. The permitting process was too complicated and costly for him to get through, and the taxes were too high for him to afford to hang on. Naturally, he went with his only option - sell out to the government. And they built a grand new recycling plant on that land.

You should travel around the countryside and see what great things the government is doing for the environment. They are running beautiful timber operations, sod farms, and landfills. They are building lakes, houses, apartment complexes, and huge corporate centers. They are doing it all with the money they force us to pay them - on the land they won't let us develop.

I knew the government was monopolizing a lot of land, but I never realized how bad things really were until we decided to put a thirty-five acre lake on our own five-hundred acre parcel. We contacted the branch of government that enforces state and federal Environmental Protection Agency (EPA) regulations in Florida. They sold us one of their maps, depicting all the protected areas on our property. And they gave us a forty-page booklet that regulated the uses of the portions of land they'd designated wetland and endangered species habitat. Since we believe in protecting the environment and had plenty of upland to use anyway, my husband and I decided not to develop the protected areas. We assumed that avoiding those areas would eliminate all the hassle with the government, and preserve the environment at the same time. Boy, were we wrong!

We had to have their permission to use any portion of our land - even the unprotected upland. And we couldn't get that permission by just agreeing to stay out of their designated areas. We had to prove their designations were right. It took several college degrees to understand their huge multi-page regulation packet, and several engineers to complete their required paperwork. The up-front application fees just to request a permit cost forty-four hundred dollars - all non-refundable, with no guarantee they'd give their blessing. And we had to have permits from six other government agencies, with similar rules, regulations, and fees.

Every agency had studies and maps, designating the areas we could not use. But instead of letting us go by their guidelines, we had to duplicate every one over and over again. We had to hire an environmental engineer to flag our wetlands, a surveyor to depict the wetland area, and a civil engineer to draw it on new maps - even though all those government agencies already had it all laid out. When government agents came out to check, they moved our flags to coincide with their maps. And our engineers had to do their work over and over again, until our studies and maps matched the government's.

The process was even more complicated because we had to go through each agency one at a time. They decided the order, and refused to cooperate with each other or coordinate their various rules and designations into one consistent set of coherent guidelines. So if we got through one, and the next disagreed with any slight specification, we had to redo and resubmit to all again. Just when we thought we were done, the last agency on the list decided they'd made a mistake by letting our driveway pass an earlier round. Because the entrance was too close to a curve in the road, they demanded that we move it fifty feet north. And since all the other permits had been issued without the new road being shown on our maps, we had to start all over again. Finally we had all the permission slips, contingent upon us building a new driveway to their specifications and paving seventy-five feet into our property from the highway - to the tune of another seventy-five thousand dollars. It took two years, $125,000, an attorney, several engineers, a soil biologist, an environmentalist, and a team of surveyors to use thirty-five acres of unregulated wasteland. And if we ever want to use any of the remaining four hundred sixty-five acres, we'll have to go back through the whole process again.

The government was a tough adversary. But my biggest battle was with myself, and with my husband. We could not afford to hold on to the land without developing it, and in fact went into debt getting through the permitting process. But I felt guilty for not standing up for the principles of freedom, and was willing to sacrifice everything to do so. My husband was not. I wanted to protest. My husband would not.

Since it is a violation of Constitutional rights to stop Americans from using their land, they don't tell you "no". They just put you through a process that makes doing so too hard and too expensive to plow through. Our project did not infringe on the environment, or one endangered species. And yet most Americans could not have afforded the excessive costs and time demands it took to get government's permission. Instead of letting us comply with all the maps and studies we taxpayers had funded, they used them to cost us money and delay. But trying to coordinate efforts with so many levels of government was the most difficult. The petty arguments between government agencies over who had the right to decide what, cost us a lot. When we had a question, no two government agents in one department could agree on the same answer.

And then there was the humiliation - people we were paying with our tax dollars and permitting fees, who had less education than we did, wielded powerful threats over our heads. And we were at their mercy. When one guy suggested that he could get us through if his son were a partner, I lost my temper. My husband ushered me from the room, and went back alone to butter him up. Jack did manage to get around him without parting with half our land, but it took several months. And to this day, I still feel guilty for not fighting the system.

Government's objective is to confiscate land, not protect the environment, nor serve its people. And if some of us don't stand up and fight, while we still have enough freedom left to do it peacefully, our children and grandchildren will never have the opportunity. The concept of saving the environment without preserving freedom along with it eludes me. Just imagine beautiful trees, animals drinking from clear running streams, eagles soaring through spacious blue skies, purple mountain majesties, and amber waves of grain - in an America where no one is free.

It's time to rain on the government's parade. Not by sacrificing the environment, but by streamlining the system. We've got to simplify the permitting process, and make the code verbiage understandable for ordinary property owners. Citizens who do not wish to dispute government maps and guidelines should be allowed to comply and follow them without having to reproduce an exact matching set. We must find a way to coordinate activities between the various government agencies, so that working with them is feasible. And to protect ourselves from unscrupulous public servants, we need to take tape recorders to our meetings with them - and I'm not kidding.

American citizens have the Constitutional right to own and control their own land. And it's time we exercised that right. As fast as Americans are losing their private property, foreigners are buying it and/or the government is taking it. It's time we stopped selling American soil to foreign investors, and auctioned what they now have back to Americans. Remember - he who owns the land controls it. And they know it. If you don't believe me, go try to buy some of theirs.

Its time we limited our government's right to land ownership - to reasonable amounts, for reasonable uses. And it's time we put the rest on the auction block, to be sold back to American citizens. The federal government alone owns over thirty million acres. And that doesn't count what all your cities, counties, and states own. In addition to all the forests, fields, waterways, and elaborate structures, these levels of government own thousands of homes all over the country - many of which are rotting from vacancy. And while too many Americans go homeless or struggle to hold on to their land, these governments are buying up more - by the thousands of acres every day.

We must stop the government from controlling and/or confiscating property that should belong to American citizens. Preserving one or two acres for every acre that we use seems fair and equitable. Even saving five for every one we use might be tolerable, if we had some clear consistent standards for all to abide by. But being forced to give the government twenty acres for the right to use every one we've bought and paid for is highway robbery. And the way the law reads now, government agents can decide to take from one to twenty-five acres for every one they agree to let us use. There are guidelines, but ultimately, much depends on what agents feel and how much they like the applicant.

Don't ever forget - he who owns the land controls it. Every time you think our government needs more of your land, remember the citizens who were evicted and barred from our national parks by the shutdown Feds. And remember those homeless refugees in countries wherein the right to property is vested with the state. Isn't it time we put forth a united effort to regain our private property, and all the other rights Americans have lost?

Put A Moratorium On Regulations

I chose the only national long distance telephone company that issued individual codes and separate bills to each real estate agent. One day our codes stopped working, and my agents had to make their call the old fashioned way - on me. I called our carrier, and learned that another long distance company had canceled our service, and switched us to theirs. I was sure there were laws against strangers messing with my business set up, and sneaking their products in on me without my knowledge or consent. So I just switched back, and refused to pay the company who interrupted my service. That company is still billing me through a collection agency, and the seventy dollar bill still stands as a blemish on my credit to this day.

When I asked how I could prevent future sabotage of this kind, I learned that the FCC still had a law against unauthorized companies switching my service, but that it had been amended to read - only if I put my name on the appropriate freeze list before the sabotage. I asked my carrier why they hadn't informed me, or encouraged me to take this protective step before I had a problem. After all, it would have kept them from losing my business even if they didn't care about me. The answer - FCC regulations had also been amended to prevent them from interfering with the competition to that extent.

Figuring I better find out what else the FCC had changed, I called for a copy of their regulations. I was told that FCC regulations had become quite complicated, and that they couldn't afford to send out all those pages of regulations to everybody any more; but that they'd be happy to send the parts relative to my problem if I could just be specific about what I needed to know. When I explained that I couldn't be sure until I checked to see what else was required of me, the agent said it sounded as though I didn't have a problem, told me to have a nice day, and hung up. Naturally, I didn't like being left in the dark, or treated so rudely by the people I pay. But I was even more outraged that the government would change a good law into something so ambiguous that nobody could benefit from it-except a sneak-thief.

Just as the regulations that control our land are too massive to plow through, the rest of the rules that govern our society are too complicated. In fact, the whole legal system is too confusing and expensive for ordinary Americans to understand, let alone trust.

The legal system we trust to protect our society from vicious criminals said O.J. Simpson was innocent of murder, yet they went after his wealth instead of the real killer. That same system that's supposed to protect the rights of the innocent ordered him to pay millions of dollars in restitution for two murders he supposedly did not commit. Then they turned around and put the care of the victim's children back in the hands of the man held monetarily responsible for stabbing her to death. Now we have no idea whether Simpson is guilty or innocent. But we do know that two people were brutally murdered, and that somebody killed them. And we know that, whether it was Simpson or someone else, the real killer is still free to strike again. What we don't know is whose son and daughter will get slashed to death the next time that murderer goes into a rage.

We've lost faith in the system's ability to provide equal justice for all. We know sexual harassment and money laundering are crimes, but no prosecuting attorney brings charges against the President or Vice President. We know it's a crime to bed fourteen-year-old kids, but the Kennedys got away with it, and probably murder. Statistics show that three thousand teenagers start smoking each day, but they go after parents and the manufacturers of legal products instead of closing the stores that violate the law. We know that too many law-abiding citizens are being fined, sued, or intimidated by an oppressive government, while too many habitual criminals go free. And we know that victims of crime suffer more than criminals.

I studied all the text material available, passed all the state-required exams, and became a licensed real estate salesperson. But I was a little too shy to sell. So I went for my instructor's and broker's licenses; then started a small real estate school. I understood the letter of the law better than those assigned to administrate and enforce it. And I trained my students accordingly. The school did pretty well. So I decided to purchase the real estate company from which I rented space. And since I believed in all those rules and regulations I taught, I had every intention of running my company in full compliance with them.

That purchase was my first actual real estate business experience. And it took me less than a month to realize that my old college professor was right.

> He said "academics and reality are a million miles apart. You can write laws, and study them till hell freezes over, but you must be a full-time villain, or the government, to get anywhere in this quagmire they call a legal system."

I purchased the whole business, including pending transactions and the escrowed trust account, from the elderly broker/owner. And she reverted to a licensed sales agent under me. She hid most of the transferred transactions, stole blank checks, and continued to close properties behind my back as if she were still the licensed broker. She even wrote checks to herself from the customer's escrow account, and kept the broker's share of the commissions.

We were both paying members of the National Association of Realtors, and her actions constituted several violations of the NAR code of ethics. The Board of Realtors took my $150 complaint filing fee, together with proof that the business and its accounts were mine, and that she had taken them. That proof included copies of our contracts, our real estate licenses, and canceled checks signed by this lady. But instead of a hearing before my peers, which was my right according to the terms of my membership agreement, they referred me to the Florida Real Estate Commission (FREC).

FREC is the government agency assigned to protect the consuming public from unscrupulous real estate agents. According to FREC licensing laws, customer funds must be held in a trust account. And it is a serious offense to tamper with them, as is stealing, dishonest dealing, and acting as a broker without a proper license. But FREC also refused to act in response to my complaint and evidence. They suggested I try criminal court, since the lady had stolen my money, stolen money held in trust for other customers, and violated several criminal fraud statutes. So I went to the local police. But they said it was a civil matter - not the kind of crime they could investigate.

Finally, I went to an attorney. He said my evidence was undeniable proof that she had violated the NAR code, FREC rules, and several criminal statutes. But after four years, and thousands of dollars in legal fees, I lost the case. My attorney had failed to file the evidence properly, and the judge threw it out. I could have filed another suit - one against my lawyer for malpractice, and maybe even one against the bank that cashed those checks. But I was too broke, and disheartened to fight another losing battle.

The sad part - I paid over $500 to get into NAR, and several hundred dollars a month for the privileges and protection of membership. Meeting FREC, and other government regulations, cost me over $2000 in start up fees, and sixty five percent of my annual income in taxes. I paid attorney fees and court costs. Yet as the victim of a crime, I still got no protection under any of the laws I lived by and paid for. After four years of being beat up mentally and financially, instead of justice or restitution, I was forced into bankruptcy.

A sadder part - even the winner lost. This lady got $25,000 down, and my promise to pay her the balance of the purchase price in monthly installments. But when I found out she was ripping me off, I stopped paying. By the time the case was settled in her favor, she'd paid her lawyer $27,000 ($2000 more than I'd given her.) Of course she was awarded the remaining $25,000 I still owed on the business, plus damages and legal fees. But a few words omitted from her lawyer's formal request for payment left me a legal loophole. I filed bankruptcy, and opened under a new corporate name that very day. With the load off my back, debt-free, and everything I'd learned as a result under my belt, I proceeded with business as usual - without ever missing a beat. And I never had to pay her another cent.

Some would say justice was served in the end. Outside of a little wear and tear, I was better off. And even though she won in court, the criminal ended up with less than she'd started with. The kind of justice we get today was served all right - the entities sworn to protect us kept their fees and dues, the judge got paid, the court got its costs, the lawyers made thousands of dollars, the criminal got to keep what she stole and never had to answer for her crime, and I got off the hook by misusing a loophole in a separate irrelevant law.

But the saddest part of all - the money taken from that escrow account belonged to some members of the consuming public. And in the real estate business, that could have been their life savings. But four levels of regulatory agencies assigned to protect the public ignored those people. Because that criminal never had to account for the money she stole, we don't know who got taken for what. I can only hope that, since no customer came forward to complain about losing hundreds of dollars, she closed their deals under the table some way, in which case my commission would have been the only thing she got away with. But she could have just as easily intimidated those customers into forfeiting their deposits. And we'll never know which she did, because the agencies assigned to protect the public didn't even ask.

Too many Americans are being forced to eat the sour grapes from this same heavy-laden vine of injustice, served on the government's expensive and dangerous platter full of control. And we're going to be eating a lot from it if we aren't careful.

We pay trillions of dollars to support a massive justice system - one which does not work much of the time. Government regulations are too many, and too ambiguous to be enforceable. Courts are too bogged down. And the legal process is too expensive to afford its people justice. We have a huge law enforcement staff, but they cannot control crime. We have a vast and overflowing prison network, but it won't hold enough criminals to keep our streets and neighborhoods safe. Laws are so complicated and confusing that good people need an attorney just to handle their daily lives. And the rules are being compounded so fast that even our own lawyers can't keep up.

As bad as all that is, there's an even darker side - the more complicated the rules become, the less we understand the system enough to challenge its authority. And when authority goes unchallenged, somebody ends up with too much power - power to line their pockets with money and freedom that should, and would otherwise be distributed among the members of society.

When prisons overflow and courts are overburdened, and leaders walk around in a cloud of suspicion in a land where most people are good and rational and sane (and we are) - it's a sure sign that power is concentrated in the hands of too few, and that the laws do not reflect the moral philosophies of the majority - especially when the majority is as reluctant to punish violent crime as we are.

Reducing our laws to a language the majority can clearly understand and be held to is of utmost importance. We must put a moratorium on regulations - at least long enough to sort through and revise the ones we already have. We must change our laws into fair and practical guidelines - ones which can be enforced. And the language of those laws must be one that ordinary citizens can read and understand.

While we're in the process of fixing the law, let's not exempt government. There is no sense making them pay taxes, since their debts come out of our pockets anyway. And of course we want to be sure the impeachment process works in our favor at every level of government. But other than that, let's hold them to the same high standards we set for ourselves and our other business. If the government can run gambling operations, so can we. If the government can build in wetlands, so can we. And if an action is a crime for us, its a crime for them too.

Except for matters of urgent national security, there is nothing more pressing for our lawmakers to do than eliminate excessive administrative costs, and make our laws much easier to understand and enforce. Let's have them get started today - and let's insist that they do nothing else until the tasks described herein are complete.

Everyone - fax, phone, or write every elected representative you have, at every level of government. Instruct them to pass no new rules or regulations until we can understand and live comfortably with the laws we have. Tell them to stop legislating new laws, and to start streamlining the old ones into making sense. And if you really want to help salvage our freedom, instruct them to keep administrative costs minimal and reduce criminal activity at the same time. And don't forget to give your lawmakers some new guidelines to follow.

Illegal Search and Seizure

Did you see that documentary on the educational channel the other night - two or three German soldiers with rifles kicking down the door and barging into that Jewish home, then herding that seven-member Jewish family into the street and off to Auschvitz? Even though the soldiers were outnumbered, that family didn't even try to grab their guns and household knives to defend themselves. When I wondered why, my husband said "What guns and knives? By the time that happened all those people had already been disarmed." That was a crime, and if we don't want it repeated here, we'd better rein in this government.

Remember when our cities first started getting crowded, and congested with crime? Because police protection was so expensive and hard to come by, we agreed to higher taxes. But robberies and vandalism continued to rise. So we agreed to five thousand new gun laws, and stayed in off the streets. As intruders broke more of our locks, the government ruled it illegal to forcibly defend anything except an open threat to our lives.

You remember those horror stories: A musician friend bought two Dobermans to guard the expensive stereo equipment stored in his second-story apartment. He posted all the normal entrances (doors) with "Beware of Guard Dogs" signs. But one night while he was out, a thief managed to climb a tree and get in through the bedroom window. Both dogs nailed the thief, and chewed him up just a little. After escaping with a few stitches and probation for attempted burglary, the intruder sued the owner for insufficient notification of a dangerous dog. That owner/

victim paid over a million dollars in damages, was fined five hundred dollars for not posting every possible entrance, and was forced to get rid of his mean dogs.

To avoid similar incidences, we moved to the suburbs. As gangs threw trash on old city streets, government regulated the size of garbage cans in our new neighborhoods. While graffiti spread across the walls of our old offices, the government mandated the lettering for our new business signs, and raised impact fees on our new buildings. And as the government extended protection for those creating decay in the city, urban ghettos begun to spread our way.

When we complained about the rising crime rate again, they passed more stringent regulations and started a campaign to stop urban sprawl - shutting off the supply of available land beyond us, and limiting land use to save the environment. The more land we conserved, the more they bought up with our tax dollars. Pretty soon much of what the government didn't buy was under their control, for the good of plants and animals.

They used our taxes to subsidize housing, then relocated the city's disadvantaged to be with us - at our expense. They forced us to give up jobs, so thieves wouldn't have to steal to eat. They increased our building safety codes to make us liable for those stoned on booze and drugs. They passed more regulations to keep us from infringing on crooks, and increased gun control laws by another five thousand so we wouldn't hurt them. They levied more taxes against us for more crime prevention programs that wouldn't work. And they gave themselves a pay raise, while we hired private security guards to protect our offices.

They increased food stamps and welfare benefits so more disadvantaged could afford transportation back and forth between our suburbs and city slums. Then they started searching cars and seizing private property along the highways to prevent drug traffic. You've heard those horror stories too - the ones that leave you scared of getting stopped on a trip. But not to worry, 'cause none of the stuff government takes ever belongs to innocent people like us - just to drug runners who haven't had their day in court yet.

Being fenced between unsuccessful crime prevention programs, failing crime control efforts, and all the bad guys was pretty scary. As the number of robberies and sexual assaults against us rose alarmingly, we moved again - into gated communities and deed-restricted subdivisions. Of course land use was more limited, and it cost us a lot more. But those funds went for a good cause - early release and rehabilitation programs that filtered criminals into our expensive new housing developments - prisons were overflowing, you know. When we protested, the government took more affirmative action - defending the criminal's Constitutional right to live wherever he wanted.

Granted, the bad guys deserved more protection than we law abiding citizens. But they did agree to warn us when murderers and child molesters moved in nearby. And that gave us the opportunity to form our own neighborhood watch patrols. As citizen watch patrols became proficient protectors, the government recruited them - gave them all the police power of an official deputy sheriff, and diverted tax dollars from crime control to provide them cruisers.

So we took the next step in home defense - bars on our windows and doors, and home security alarm systems. But the crime rate continued to soar. So the government devoted more taxes and police protection to ineffective safety programs. They bought up most of the vacant land so wild animals wouldn't threaten our neighborhoods. They removed citizens from slippery streets up north to keep them from becoming fallen prey. They banned cigarettes in most public places so we could smell the stench of weed. They made kids wear bike helmets to keep their heads from getting bashed in. They started curtailing nighttime activity so we wouldn't be exposed to the dark. Finally, they're coming after the bad guys - right through the iron bars on our windows and doors. And our security alarms are blaring a warning: "American citizen, you've got no place else left to go."

The government has finally come up with a rational excuse to enter our homes at will - without knocking and without a search warrant. At this very moment Congress, together with several state governments, are drafting the regulations under which they will be entitled to enter private homes for the purpose of searching for and seizing illegal drugs. They claim that in order to stop the flow and halt drug-related crimes, they must have the advantage of surprise-attack. They say when cops knock, too many criminals flush their drugs and escape out the back - shooting uniformed public servants as they go.

On the surface it appears to make sense. But then so did searching our cars. I don't know about you, but I'd rather provide policeman more bullet proof vests and riot helmets than give them the key to my house. Surely by now we know we have more to fear from government's bursting into our homes than we do from criminals. Surely we won't let the government scare us into giving them more control. Surely we see that no matter how much we give, or how many rights we concede, crime will never be controlled until the people are empowered to protect themselves.

We've given up control of our cities and businesses. We've forfeited the right to freely use our land. Our property can be searched and seized on the open road without provocation. Our legal use of firearms has practically been regulated into extinction. And we've still had to bar our windows and doors. The last thing we need is a bunch of strange cops with our house keys.

Before you decide to let these people burst through your front door, ask yourself a few questions. How many cops on your local police force would you trust to reign over you? And how many government agents do you want entering your home without knocking? Who are these authorities anyway? Some are probably good guys, but I know too many who aren't. And it's so easy to impersonate today. At best, these public servants are just as human as we are - maybe a little better-trained, but no smarter, and no more moral. Most of them skipped college. And when you get right down to the bare facts, too many aren't exactly the cream of the crop. Whether we like to admit it or not, we cannot always trust them. Too many are real serious power freaks and thrill seekers. Some have less-than-pure motives, and others are definitely on the take. A few are downright abusive.

Maybe you had better write your congressman a protesting letter - today.

DEREGULATE THE INNOCENT

Our hearts ache for the Bradys of the world, the Simpson-Goldman families, Oklahoma City, and school kids across our nation. Legislators, together with irate citizens, tried to stop their kind of pain - by eradicating firearms. But the more the Bradys fought and won wars against guns, the higher the crime rate soared. Why? Because it wasn't a gun, or the rights of the law-abiding citizens carrying a gun, that disabled Jim Brady - it was the criminal who pulled the trigger. And nobody has done a thing to stop him.

Any good psychologist will tell you that we must set clear and definite limits on bad behavior, while allowing as much freedom to do good as possible. With "innocent until proven guilty" running ever utmost through our minds and laws, we must revamp the system so that it works in favor of the good guys. We must redefine crime to reflect the true profile of criminals, and adjust our laws accordingly. We must concentrate on nabbing criminals and making them pay, instead of regulating ourselves, and/or the tools we use.

Preventive laws, aimed at keeping honest people honest, have no effect on criminals. Sacrificing the rights and freedoms of law-abiding citizens, and giving government and law enforcement power over good people does nothing to interfere with the activities of bad guys.

And here comes the President again - insisting that the only way to beat the drug problem in America is to be able to enter our homes for the purpose of searching and seizing, without knocking and without a search warrant. I know the President believes history belongs in the past. But forfeiting our Constitutional right to privacy puts our national heritage too far back to suit me. Our founding fathers must be rolling over in their graves. I know my Dad is.

Just remember - "as the rights of the majority go, so go the rights of everybody else in the country." When the rights of criminals take priority over law abiding citizens, nobody is safe. And when law-abiding citizens are forced to give up their freedoms because of the criminal activities of a few, nobody is free.

Keep in mind that governments do not make our deeds right or wrong. And just because a law is on the books does not mean it's fair. Remember when slavery was legal, and they used to burn witches at the stake? Remember when it was a crime for women and minority citizens to vote? It took a lot of people power to get things changed back then, and it will take even more to make the kind of changes we need today.

The message "deregulate the innocent" must get through to our law makers. And it must be heavy laden with some mighty plain directives - like "get rid of all laws that turn normal activities into criminal offenses. Restore the rights of American citizens. And don't even think about invading the privacy of our homes, or our automobiles on the highway ever again."

Sensible laws don't handicap law-abiding citizens. So we must insist that they restore our right to bear arms and protect ourselves, restore our private property rights and our right to discipline our children, fix our roofs, and walk our streets at night, to run our businesses as free enterprises, to choose our own friends and associates, and all the other rights guaranteed us by our Constitution - all of which they have taken away. And don't let them kid you - they don't have to mess with the Constitution to do it. All they have to do is remove the quagmire under which they've buried our Constitutional freedoms.

The Constitution of the United States of America instructs that no state or lower branch of government infringe on the rights she guarantees. And that Constitution prohibits the overbearing and oppressive amount of control it takes for government to save us from every sin. Yet at least five subordinate levels of government, (each with departments and commissions and divisions and boards and agencies of it's own), pass thousands of laws every week, aimed at regulating our moral and ethical conduct. It takes pages and pages of complicated and confusing legal verbiage, with a million loopholes in every one, for these moral and ethical laws to avoid conflict with the Constitution. And the result is a tangled web of unenforceable and meaningless rules and regulations that intimidate all good people into submission, while protecting none of them from anything. As my Dad would say - "Laws that do nothing but keep honest people honest." We need to sort through and discard every rule and law that violates our basic Constitutional rights.

Liberty only has to be granted once, to make it so. And a law only needs written down once, to be a crime. Yet millions of ambiguous repetitive regulations are duplicated over and over again at all these various levels of government. Each level writes their own version - each with a little different slant, of course. And every time they change the language, the waters of freedom get a little muddier. By the time it reaches us, nobody knows what they're allowed to do, or not do. This redundant waste of paper destroys an awful lot of those priceless tress we're trying to save - and the oxygen they produce might be just the amount needed to carry us through global warming. Let's get rid of the government's wasteful redundancy, and save those trees.

We can further lighten the load for good citizens by instructing our lawmakers to eliminate all the rules and regulations, administrative codes, and ethical codes of conduct implemented by any department or commission or agency that has not been directly elected by the people. A support staff to help elected representatives gather and sort data is fine. But our elected representatives aren't even at work ninety percent of the time. And the outfits they appoint to do their jobs are so buried that we can't reach them with our vote. The ballot box is our only means of balancing the power. And appointing all these officials to regulate us amounts to taxation and regulation without elected representation. Every principle we stand for opposes that.

It's time to let your congressman know you're paying him to keep you free.

Revamp The Justice System

In addition to smothering liberty and trashing our free enterprise system, the quagmire of confusing regulations passed to date renders most violations unprovable and unenforceable. It ties the hands of our law enforcement officers when we need them, yet can't stop them when they get out of control. It makes conviction harder on the victim than it is on the criminal and restitution impossible to achieve. It bogs down our courts and leaves us all at the mercy of attorneys. It breeds the kind of apathy and disrespect that fosters lawlessness, social unrest, and disorder within our society. And justice is rarely served.

The protection of our society depends on being able to gather enough evidence to warrant arresting the bad guy quickly. And arrests must be based on factual evidence, not on police instincts or press coverage. But we seem to be failing to get at those facts. We've stayed on the President's case for over six years, and still haven't gathered enough evidence to make an arrest. We've left the Simpson case, along with too many other high-profile murders, unsolved. We've even stooped to Gestapo-type tactics, like the harassment of Jewels after the Olympic bombing in Atlanta. And criminals are still roaming the streets.

We've got the most elaborate high-tech equipment, the most expensive operating budget, and the largest enforcement team in the world. We've got everything from complex chemical analysis and DNA testing, to all the experts we need to clarify the results for us. If all that can't produce a better arrest record, we're either after the wrong guys, or we need a new team of investigators. But then gathering evidence is not the problem - getting the uncontaminated facts in front of a jury is.

Take that business purchase I got ripped off on - the forged checks had the name of my business printed on their face. Ownership was indisputably spelled out in the contract, and proven by payments I made. The date of transfer was confirmed by FREC-required forms, bank records, and state licenses issued. And I had the checks with the thief's signatures on them in my hand, stamped on the back after they'd passed through my trust account. I had plenty of evidence. But I couldn't get far enough around the legal maneuvering for anybody to see it. And it wasn't like I hadn't started soon enough, or tried hard enough.

We need to make evidence more readily available. It's time we replaced irrelevant time lines and legal maneuvering in the courtroom with the presentation of facts. It's time we got a chance to examine legally-gathered information relative to the crime before it gets tainted by age and bureaucratic screw-ups. Legal maneuvers may present attorneys an opportunity to strut their stuff and make more money. But legal maneuvers are not facts. And they do nothing to clear the way for determining true innocence or guilt. They just confuse the issues.

Besides, a society being victimized by crime is just as innocent as the accused, and deserves just as much protection. Many of our laws can be rewritten to be reasonable and fair to both sides without infringing on anybody's rights. For instance, the time line - just as defendants need time to prepare against sudden attack, society needs to present factual evidence that turns up late. A little more control over lawyers and judges will help to accommodate both.

And since the protection of a free society requires the presumption of innocence until proven guilty, we must remember that those tied up in the investigative process are not criminals. Even after being arrested, they are innocent until and unless they have been convicted in court. And part of "due process" is their right to a speedy trial.

How many times was O.J. Simpson publicly convicted and acquitted before he finally got a trial, and before he was declared innocent? And then there was Timothy McVeigh - shackled in prison for two years before he ever got his day in court. When a foreign country ransacks the private abodes of the innocent like Jewels, or shackles a dissident in prison for two years before deciding his fate, we accuse them of deliberately persecuting political prisoners. Have Americans stooped that low? Two years in shackles, waiting to be heard, is right out of the Dark Ages, as is harassment based on suspicion.

A system so encumbered by legal maneuvering, or so bogged down with people in trouble that it can't bring the accused to trial within a reasonable period of time, can never serve anybody justice. It will either victimize the unfairly accused, or leave the rest of us in danger; and there's no way to know which until a jury hears the facts. In a free country, right and wrong shouldn't have so many ambiguities and gray areas - and when it does, gray should definitely equal "free and innocent."

As good citizens, we need to trust ourselves as jurors, and trust our verdicts. The ordinary people of this country are not deaf, dumb, or blind. And before the government decides we aren't capable or deserving of other liberties, we'd better start proving it. It's time we got excited about sitting on our juries, instead of thinking of ways to get off. It is our civic duty.

Of course we cannot afford to be locked away from our families and jobs for weeks and months at a time to ponder evidence, and we shouldn't have to be. Believe it or not, we can make fair and rational judgments without being sequestered under armed guard, in spite of all the propaganda they feed us. So let's get rid of the rules that make it too hard for good citizens to do their share. We may not be perfect, but unless our relatives are on trial, we are capable of serving on the jury as our names are drawn. Holding up due process through months of legal maneuvering designed to remove jurors who might not vote one way or the other will not change the facts of any case. And limiting our participation in the justice process because we might have pre-formed personal opinions is nothing more than a tactic to stifle free thinking. We are capable of following the rules, sorting fact from fiction and personal prejudice, and rendering fair verdicts - in a timely fashion.

After a speedy trial, we must insist on immediate release of the innocent, and swift effective punishment for those convicted. Our legal system has grown so many side bars that we can't trust it to protect us anymore. That was particularly evident throughout O.J. Simpson's three trials of the century. Remember - the jury system that's supposed to protect our society from vicious criminals declared Simpson innocent. That same system that's supposed to protect the innocent ordered him to pay millions of dollars in restitution for murders he supposedly didn't commit. And then that same system we entrust to make judgments on our behalf put the care of those children back in the hands of the man held monetarily responsible for stabbing their mother to death!

We heard all kinds of excuses as to why: law enforcement and prosecutors botched the case; the racial make up of the two different colored juries reflected each one's prejudices; civil trails are people-oriented and freer to gather and use evidence, whereas government oriented criminal trials are too restricted." To restricted to do what - assure society justice?

To me, it all sounded like more emotional manipulation designed to justify sending more government control our way. Aren't all our courts people-oriented? They should be. And since when does the color of one's skin render a person incapable of deciphering facts? Aren't you all a little afraid of such an incompetent law-enforcement agency, and even more afraid of a government that can twist your people-oriented laws into a system that can continue to punish and ruin you for something your peers say you didn't do?

We must eliminate the double jeopardy of civil court. Since lawyers get to steal our wallets twice (once for society, and again when the victim sues for damages) we're going to have to really push this point. Remind them that a crime against one of us is a crime against all, and vice versa. If an offense is not serious enough to be considered a crime, or criminal evidence is not relevant enough to stand in the courts designed to protect all against evil, then it isn't serious enough to cause the financial ruination and public humiliation of any American.

Those two types of Simpson trials, civil and criminal, with two different verdicts made a mockery out of our justice system. They cast a shadow of motivational doubt over the families of the victims, and scrved all of America injustice. If we continue to make the innocent pay financially, while killers go free, it won't be long until we'll all be victims - if not of the criminal, for sure of the government. If our public servants can't do a better job, we need to replace them. If our courts cannot protect our society and provide its wounded restitution, we need to fix them, not duplicate them.

We need one set of simple laws with penalties that fit the crime, and one court system that will consistently uphold them. How 'bout starting with this: "Thou shalt not deliberately kill or inflict bodily harm on, or steal from, or deal dishonestly with another human being. And if someone makes you do so, your punishment shall be theirs also. If restitution for your unjust deed is possible, you shall be given opportunity to make it right. If you are a temporary threat to society, you shall be jailed until you can be trusted, at which time your assets and the assets you accumulate thereafter shall be confiscated and given to your victim until full restitution is made. If restitution and/or the protection of the community is not possible, as in murder and rape and extreme bodily harm, you will be eliminated for the good of all the society, by either life imprisonment or death."

Those are simple rules. And contrary to popular belief, anyone who doesn't know what it means to deliberately kill, injure, steal, and deal dishonestly shouldn't be free on our streets anyway. If our children don't understand, we must educate them quickly. Those among us who are dangerously-impaired mentally must be confined and watched over - for their sakes, as well as society's. And the rest of us will have to learn to cope with our heartaches and deal with our hang-ups instead of using them as an excuse to vent on society and then avoid prosecution.

It's Time Crime Didn't Pay

Sensible laws and a fair system are not enough to protect our society. We need education, and a system of punishment that deters crime. Present day educational programs and other crime-prevention tactics do not work. They may teach that crime doesn't pay, but too many real-life role models prove that academic theory to be wrong. Rehabilitative programs forced on previous offenders usually fail because those who have already had experience with the system know it is not all that painful. True justice requires swift and effective punishment, and penalties severe enough to deter wrongful deeds.

Granted, we are incapable of creating a perfect society at the moment, and we could make a mistake. But when justice is served from the hands of twelve law-abiding citizens, odds are we'll get it as right as humanly possible. Those odds diminish considerably when criminals and governments are allowed to run the show. We must learn to trust our guilty verdicts, and hand out immediate punishment. And again - that may mean changing the way we think.

Believe it or not, in a learned civilized community, justice is not about prevention or love, even though we are filled with sparing compassion. It is not about paying lawyers and empowering government, even when we have the money to do so. It is not about regulating good citizens and mindless products, although we have to practice self restraint. And it is not about revenge and punishment, even though we must use them as tools to deter crime.

Justice among the learned and civilized is about protecting society, and assuring its injured victims restitution. Today we restrain ourselves, and coddle criminals until their crimes outrage us, or hit too close to home. Then, out of anger and fear, we rush to demand that somebody pay. But the objective of true justice is to protect society and its members - not to punish or seek revenge. Therefore, we must redirect our efforts toward gaining something for society and its wounded, instead of inflicting pain on the offender.

Remember Susan Smith - the girl who drowned her little boys in North Carolina? Nothing Susan Smith could be forced to endure would restore life to those kids, or ease the pain of those who loved and lost them. The prosecutor, knowing there was no possibility of getting restitution for the victims, went after the only other thing he understood - revenge. And the defense attorney used that vengeful motive to save her life. He persuaded the jury that living life in prison, haunted by the fact that she had killed her own children, would be worse for her than death; and therefore, she was spared execution.

The first mistake was believing people like Susan Smith are haunted the way we perceive being haunted. Of course, the thought of having to live with ourselves after committing such a horrible crime against the children we love seems unbearable. But then, we wouldn't dream of drowning our kids. Yes, we all make regrettable mistakes, but not to this degree. And those who do are either too ill or too unconscionable to dwell among the civilized. Until we face these realities, the vast majority of our people will not be safe.

Our goal must be to protect society - not to inflict pain on an offender. What will Smith's vengeful penalty really accomplish? Well, if she serves the max, life in prison will further burden the society that must support her. But under our current system, she'll be out for sure in fifteen years; and given rehabilitation under an early-release program, she'll probably be out in five. Either way, she'll be unleashed upon society again. Before she's forty, she'll be free and rich - equipped with an education at the taxpayer's expense and the opportunity to sell her story for millions. She may even have more children to harm. That's neither revenge nor social justice. In fact, given her circumstances, that isn't even punishment. If we had focused on true justice for society and its members instead of revenge, we'd have eliminated the financial burdens and physical threats associated with harboring this mad woman in our midst.

I know that's another harsh statement, and I can just hear the outrage coming from religious leaders, the scientific community, and lawyers everywhere. But one set of their books is just as confusing and ambiguous as the next, and none of them make any sense. The preacher's Bible says everything from "Thou shalt not kill," and "Turn the other cheek," to "An eye for and eye." Yet more wars are fought, and more clinics are bombed by Christian right-to-lifers than by any other group on this planet. Science books run the gamut from bleeding heart excuses for rehabilitating killers to assisted suicide and then back to survival of the fittest. Law books give both life and death the benefit of the doubt, and each lawyer pulls out whichever emotional scripture suits his pocketbook at any given time - while we, the society and all our injured members, are victimized and overwhelmed by all the crime.

Don't misunderstand me - I'm not necessarily an advocate of the death penalty, abortion, euthanasia, or any other taking of a human life. Here, I'm just as torn over right and wrong as you are. But as I watch so many innocents (especially children) being zapped by criminals and psychopaths, I know we've got to make some difficult decisions. And one of them has to be eliminating those who endanger our society. Whether that means the death penalty, or life in prison with bread and water - the majority will have to decide. But if we don't get criminals and lunatics off the streets, none of us will survive.

What did McVeigh's justice do for society, and/or its wounded members? Whether McVeigh was innocent or guilty, two years in shackles was a tremendous expense to taxpayers, while his lawyers made a fortune on preparation and legal maneuvering. And while government and lawyers profited by denying that citizen due process, society sat on the edge - not knowing whether the guilty party was behind bars, or if the real culprit was out there somewhere making another bomb. Of course, government continued to provide their usual measure of preventive medicine - hundreds of new regulations that trampled our freedoms for fear there were more terrorists dwelling among us. And now we are feeding and clothing and sheltering the man who destroyed our property, defiled our land, and maimed or slaughtered over one hundred of our people. Some of us are wondering if the government set him up, while others live in fear that appeals will eventually put him back on our streets. And while restitution and justice continue to elude society, the victims of McVeigh's crime must pay for his keep.

We must not be so reluctant to punish violent crimes. Appeals based on new and real evidence is one thing. But the truth, just because it's spoken out of turn, is no excuse to set a murderer free, or allow him to avoid punishment for years. Neither society nor its wounded members should be forced to support a criminal while he writes his memoirs. If death is what it is to be, then immediately it should be so. And if the decision is life, the burden and risk to society must be minimized.

A system that goes soft on offenders is as much to blame for a soaring crime rate as the bad guys are. Crime is deterred by punishing criminals - not by rewarding them. The word "prison" must be redefined - and not as a free ride in the amusement park, or a new business location supported by the taxpayer. Since criminals are not law-abiding citizens, they have no right to the privileges of such - no inmates filing law suits or voting, or accumulating assets in the outside world while behind bars.

Too many inmates enjoy a better standard of living than those of us who are working hard and paying their overhead. How 'bout a mandatory work detail for every prisoner - at least eight hours a day, five days a week, without pay, for the city, county, state, or Feds who have them locked up? Prisoners would be too busy to run businesses that scam us from their cells. And they'd get their exercise without us having to provide gyms and entertainment. Plus - they'd be paying their own way for a change. If they escape, reduce their bread and water when we find them - if they can't be contained under armed guard long enough to pay their own keep, they don't deserve much.

Training and rehabilitation should only be available to inmates truly capable of becoming self-sufficient members of society, and only if they are willing to work their way through school. All privileges should be forfeited, including candy bars, telephones, and personal television sets. Television programs should be limited anyway, just so they aren't exposed to any more violent ideas. Killers and thieves and rapists should consider themselves lucky to be given a roof over their heads, a bed, enough to curb their hunger pains, a uniform, and an opportunity to pay for it all. Realistically, maybe they should just be served the humane needle of death.

Parolees should be few and far between. If the sentence is too harsh, don't hand it out. And if it fits, let them do their time. Prisons may be crowded for a little while. But getting rid of the luxury space will automatically create more room. And as rumors of criminals being punished instead of pampered start to spread, an awful lot of those defying nature to get into the criminal justice system will find something more productive to do.

Besides clamping down on the bad guys, streamlining the laws to exclude those who don't belong in prison will ease the burdens of our overloaded courts, and the overcrowding in our prisons. Normal activities won't be challenged in court anymore. Justice will be served at criminal sentencing, so victims won't have to go back to civil court for restitution. And when the punishment fits the crime, white collar offenders, con artists, and other non violent thieves won't be in jail - they'll be out making restitution.

Remember - we're doing what's best for society and its wounded members here. So restitution must be paid to the damaged party, and must be consistent with the amount lost. That won't turn the pauper who got taken for ten bucks into a millionaire. But neither will it allow the bad guy to live in a big house on the hill while paying back peanuts. And one hundred hours of community service won't be enough to compensate taxpayers who have been stripped of thousands of dollars. If this is to work, we need some real payback - to the people who really suffer loss. If we keep the language of the law simple, and leave out the loopholes, it won't be as complicated as it sounds. Besides, by the time we're done, the white collar crime rate will drop drastically. And we won't have that many scoundrels to house in jail.

Many of the rules and regulations that violate our Constitutional rights also serve to entrap good people. They carry an assumption of guilt rather than innocence. So even if you're falsely accused, it's easier and cheaper to admit guilt and pay than it is to fight. If you get ripped off, it's easier and cheaper to chalk your losses up to a learning experience than to pursue justice. So shysters, banking on the fact that we'd rather pay than fight, play the numbers game - and win ninety percent of the time. Streamlining the laws into making sense will eliminate a lot of the angles they use to dupe us. When the angles are gone from the law, the shysters will begin to fade away. And we'll be wise to the ones that don't.

You know that system the government uses to notify citizens when a sex offender moves into their neighborhood- well, we won't need it anymore. When criminal rights no longer take precedence over the rights of law-abiding citizens and true justice is served, those predators will either be in prison or socially outcast from our midst. So instead of alerting us as to the whereabouts of perverts, the government can alert us to the activities and presence of nonviolent thieves. When faced with social humiliation, declining profits and real payback, these scoundrels (private and government crooks alike) will practically disappear too.

Ending Government's Bad Business Practices

A private company was paying us for empty cans, plastics, and old papers; and we were recycling just fine. Then along came the county, claiming we weren't doing enough. They issued a mandate for citizens to recycle, and tougher rules for the private recycling companies. They started building a new public recycling plant at the taxpayers' expense, on land they wouldn't allow a private owner to develop. On the day it opened, they gave every citizen green recycling bins (thanks taxpayers); and promised not to charge for picking them up. They also gave citizens free exemption forms (thanks again taxpayers), to be filled out by the private recycler you could choose to use. Then they updated the recycling rules - any citizen who didn't have the county's green bin on the curb on the designated pick up day would have to show their exempt form, or risk being fined.

Now the county didn't order private industry out of business. But they made it so easy to use their recycling service, and so complicated not to, that most of us switched for convenience's sake. Without our trash, the private competition soon folded. The county couldn't afford to pay citizens for their trash, like the private recyclers did. And the day the private competition went out of business, every property owner got hit with a small recycling fee - seventy-five dollars to help recover the county's loss was added to their property taxes once a year.

Isn't it amazing? The private recycler paid all his own start-up costs and overhead, paid us for our trash, and still made a profit. The taxpayer purchased everything the county needed, from land to trucks; the citizens were bullied into giving government their recyclable materials, and even paid an extra charge to cover overhead - and the county still can't show a profit. But we do have to give the government some credit. They bought all new trucks (thanks again and again taxpayers), and provided jobs to the drivers laid off by the closed down private competition.

And look what they're doing to the tobacco companies - well some of them anyway. The state of Florida owns $950,000,000 worth of tobacco company stock - but not in the companies it joined with other states to sue. I am afraid of a government that threatens to take custody of our children if we smoke around them, while investing so much of our money in the company that supposedly does us so much harm. Does that make sense to you? And even more frightening - lawyers for the states offered tobacco companies immunity from private suits, so long as the companies gave the government entities being represented a considerable sum of money, and more control - like they had the power to trade off our damages.

Between government propaganda and the passage of new rules, the government managed to ban smoking in most places, and restrict the rest. But the thing that irked me the most - when private entrepreneurs agreed to cooperate with nonsmokers, by opening up separate establishments that catered to smokers, the government said no. And if you think the medical bills were high before, wait till you see the cost of new affirmative action programs aimed at rehabilitating smokers. The tobacco companies are fighting back though. And as bad as we hate smoking, we'd better get behind them - for they are one of the few free enterprise organizations left, with enough money and clout to win. When they prove freedom can win, most other private companies will follow suit.

Free enterprise is being jeopardized by our government more and more every day. Uncle Sam is our largest competitor. And all his cousin-departments have the perfect pattern for expansion down pat. They buy and prepare land, then build whatever facility they want on it, at our expense.

They work it out so that they end up with unlimited cash flow, no regulations to contend with, and the ability to control the market.

At home the government's business operations are so massive, they make our largest corporations look like small mom and pop shops. And there are millions of government rules and regulations aimed at stifling we, the American free and enterprising citizen-competitors. Bureaucratic business operations cost taxpayers trillions of dollars. And they are run by people who are neither elected by nor qualified to represent us. These agents use their position to monopolize, wield power over the heads of the people they serve, and squelch those they cannot exploit.

They whip up the waters against private companies, by exaggerating or creating bad publicity, then clamp down on private companies for each citizen's own good - with a mandate that squeezes the private guy out. The changeover is so smooth and easy we never know he's gone. A few-dollar price hike gets tacked on to our tax bill at the end of each year. Friendly customer service just seems to disappear, right along with efficient operations and profits. And we never seem to notice - until the market is held captive and consumers are under control.

If you think government's takeover of this nation's private enterprises is in the best interest of the people, try getting some friendly quality service from the ones they already run. Then examine your tax bill to see if you're paying double for the products government sells. And while you're at it, check their labels for limitations on use - if you have time to read through themess.

If you believe socialism is fairer and better, try living on social security today without any extra supplemental income. And keep in mind that when the government talked of budget cuts, they never mentioned giving up foreign aid or their limousines and big salaries - just welfare and social security. Now tell me you want them to take over the whole economy.

Eighty-five percent of American businesses have under six employees. I own one of them. And if you own one, you know how much the government charges to let you stay open. Together, we owner/managers of these small businesses provide hundreds of thousands of Americans with jobs. We spend half our sixteen-hour-long days dealing with government regulations. We pay sixty-five percent of our gross income out in taxes and regulatory fees, and then pay another thirty-three percent on the personal income we take home. If you don't believe me, count it up - income tax, utility tax, sales tax, special assessment tax, property tax, capital gains, intangible tax, corporation fees, all the different permits and licensing fees, several miscellaneous taxes and fees at seven separate levels of government.

And while we are being indoctrinated to save the whole world, but not our own souls, the government is getting bigger and more powerful around the globe. Alan Greenspan (U. S. Federal Reserve Chairman) referred to the international financial system as a new regime. He said we do not yet understand it well enough to accurately predict its repercussions, but that he knows it needs a more powerful committee to provide better supervision.

I know we have problems to solve, but the government can't solve them. Even when they try, things don't get resolved in our favor. Look what they've done to our schools and our legal system. Remember when we used to be able to buy decent hospitalization - the kind that let us choose our own doctors. That was before government decided to go into the insurance business. Doctors used to be dedicated to healing the sick, and their incomes used to depend on a good reputation for doing so. Now there's Medicare and Medicaid, and payment from the government every time we have to go back. No wonder there's no cure for anything under twenty thousand dollars.

Government regulated real estate until they had more subsidized housing programs than Century 21; and thousands of those homes and apartment complexes are still rotting from vacancy, while a lot of Americans go homeless. Government regulated savings and loans into bankruptcy, and then charged the taxpayer to bail them out. You paid for your house; you helped buy houses for about fifty million people who didn't pay their bills; then you paid the Resolution Trust Corporation (RTC) to take over the savings and loans companies, and confiscate a lot of property from people like those Clinton and McDougal ripped off. And what did you get for it - FDIC insurance wrapped in several new layers of bureaucracy, with substantially less coverage to protect whatever little savings you had left.

And think what you got from welfare reform? You heard the President instruct all government agencies to find positions for those being forced off welfare by the new reforms. He never said "if we have openings" or "if they are qualified". In fact, he never even mentioned those points. I thought the objective of welfare reform was to release hard working Americans from unfair burdens - not to increase the government's payroll, and render it less efficient than it already is.

Now the feds are taking over telecommunications and broadcasting, because air waves are getting too crowded. And the Federal Communications Commission (FCC) is going to oversee transmissions. Finally, a bomb shell exploding too close to home - being forced to replace all my television sets by the year 2000. I haven't been this wide awake and mad for years - not since Dad and I sat up watching Americans sacrifice themselves to snakes and rats. And they want to go global across the airwaves.

Maybe there are no red flashing lights in your windows of opportunity, but I hear sirens echoing from my Daddy's past. Maybe free enterprise as we know it will not come to a screeching halt before the end of the twentieth century. But what if it does? We've already given up our right to operate our businesses here at home to government supervision - for fear we would discriminate against each other, or take advantage of someone, or keep too much of our profits, or fail to share enough with the needy. And our own government is bankrupting and taking over our businesses faster than we can close up shop. What if the new global regime and its powerful new committee fears we might discriminate against the world or take advantage of someone overseas? What if they decide to keep our profits, and make us share more? How fast will they close us down if they don't get what they want? Have they started already?

Granted, there are still a few large companies making it big here. But for every one of them that's stayed, five have moved out of the country. Steel is long gone. Check out the labels on your clothing, plastics, ceramics, and electronics. Find out where your car and computer was made. Even a lot of our food is now being shipped in - since our government subsidizes most American farmers, and controls most of the land we used to grow crops on.

It's not that I don't want to purchase legitimate government service or trade in the world's market. I just want to take it slow and careful - careful enough to stay in control of my own destiny. I don't want to risk having to feed the nation's children from the world's case of powdered milk mixed with overseas shells. And I'm not so sure we can dig out from under a whole world of bureaucracy to save them. We're already having trouble unloading the wagon full of crap we have right here at home.

I don't know about you, but as for me and mine - we say "No thank you, Uncle Sam, we're passing up control by you and every other global regime." Fortunately a lot of other Americans are joining with us. If you'd like to come along, don't bring a shovel. The act of passing is simple - just eliminate the government's competition over here, and stop buying foreign products being shipped in from over there.

Yes, it will probably hurt economically at first. But Americans have never had much trouble recovering. If the bottom falls out while we're in control, we'll just start over and rebuild. Just think of all the new opportunities - new jobs galore, and Americans helping each other trade services again. That's sure a lot better than waiting for government (ours or the world's) to pull the rug out from under us. When government wins an economic war, training centers house kids who aren't old enough to work, the old and incapacitated are eradicated, and the rest of the civilian population toil in labor camps. And don't forget - the world doesn't give kids as many years to grow up as we do.

Some of you think there's more risk in holding back than there is in plunging forward - and for good reason. I know the economy appears to be doing great, with the Feds running the show. But the last time I checked, the interest gained on my savings account was a lot less than what I pay on my credit card. And some people I know are charging because they don't have anything saved. Most young couples are so busy working that they don't even have time to think about being free. How many hours are you and your spouse putting in to keep up?

And when was the last time you felt you got your money's worth - when your dad stood up and screamed a long time ago? It's hard to find quality products and good services. We can't trust most of the people we do business with and we don't have time to read all the fine print attached to everything we buy. My glasses need a stronger prescription every time it shrinks, and I keep going back to school to learn each new language it's written in.

You worry about stepping on Uncle Sam's toes, 'cause you know he's holding up the stock market. You know he's the nations largest employer, and that he controls most of the businesses and the services we need. And you know he wants to go global with all that power and wealth. How many times have you been laid off because your company had to down-size or move? And how many Stress-tabs did you take today? When you glance at an old German or Russian documentary, do you wish you could take a few more? Of course you do. We all know we're being lulled into a sense of false security. And we're all just a little bit scared.

You think the good old U.S.A. is too crowded to handle another boom. We say drive around the countryside and check out the wide open spaces. You think we don't have enough land left to grow our own crops. We want to stay free enough to farm out the leftovers. You think our soil is all worn out. We know we have more than any other country. You think you'll have to pay more for homemade stuff. We want rid of government control and foreign influences so the free market system can bring our prices back into line.

You don't want to destroy any more of our environment. But we now know how to protect it as we use it; and governments are exempt from doing that. Besides, we're already paying to protect the rain forests in South America, the elephants in Africa and India, the oil fields in the Mid East, and you name it - and we don't even have to depend on them yet. How much do you think they'll wrench us for when we do?

You know most Americans are already working, and wonder where we'll get the labor pool. We could give our handicapped and elderly a rest. And look at the poverty rate - I bet, if we started offering a little job security again, a lot of the homeless and hungry would come in off the streets. Besides, cutting back the size and reach of government will free up a pretty large work force.

You think Americans have been gluttons too long, and fear that the rest of the world will start demanding a bigger share. I say Americans don't take kindly to threats nor lies. Free enterprise may never be utopia, and a few less capable may suffer while most prosper. But under government control, everybody is less capable and everybody suffers - except the few in charge at the top. And you can be sure that what foreigners now label "the shameful greedy fruits from our labors" will quickly turn into a "well-deserved bounty" once the new global regime gets their hands on it. The truth is - a hell of a lot more of the world will go hungry, if Americans lose charge of feeding them. But we won't.

We're too wide awake and mad to let government suppress our ability to excel and prosper. We're smart enough to know that the world's oppressed count on us to produce, and that we cannot give them what we do not have. We're too compassionate to abandon the hungry and homeless for long. We are brave, strong, wealthy, and still free - and most importantly, we are going to make sure we stay that way.

You and I - we own this American government; it doesn't own us. That means that running it is our business, and we get to call the shots. Every government employee is on our payroll. And that means they have to do the sucking up, not us. Of course we're not the type to flaunt our power. But we do have good business heads on our shoulders, and we're going to start using them. Just like our Daddies always said we could - we'll dream the dream, and then make it come alive.

We're going to unite, and take back control of our government. Because the paper trail has gotten too long, we know the system needs a complete regulatory overhaul. We'll rewrite the laws of our land to reflect the freedoms guaranteed us by the Constitution. We'll redefine and capture crime, reclaim our land, and make the streets within our communities safe once again. We'll reclaim our children, take back control of our schools, and educate our nation as to the meaning of liberty. We'll take back our businesses, demand that our products return to the highest quality, and set good citizens free to thrive and grow prosperously.

We know that if taxes and administrative costs bankrupt the majority, the whole nation will live in poverty and oppression. And we are not about to let that happen. So we'll eliminate the waste and cut the taxes that support it. With profits and paychecks back in hand, we'll feed our hungry and shelter the homeless. And we'll support the present generation, while preserving enough of our environment to last for generations to come.

Because our management team is way out of line, government is costing too much and helping too little. So we'll do some restructuring within the personnel department. Our objective is clear - a few good people who will concentrate on preserving our liberties, while we prosper and thrive in the free-world market, and continue to share that prosperity with the less fortunate at home and abroad.

We'll insist that our government managers streamline every department, and eliminate all those that do not provide a truly necessary government service. We'll remove our government from the world's trading centers, and set up our own shops there. We'll take government out of the utility business, out of the real estate industry, out of the medical profession, out of loan-sharking, out of the import business, out of the insurance business, and out of the trash business- and put Uncle Sam, together with all his state and county and city cousins, back to work for the American people.

Under our administrative shadow, government agents will be afraid to waste and overspend. We'll get rid of wretched leaders who don't support good citizenship and free enterprise. And we'll save money doing it - by getting rid of all the unnecessary personnel and personal assistants. We'll replace any staff member who proves to be unqualified, or unable to follow directions. And we'll accept no more excuses. If an employee can't do his job, we'll replace him with someone who can.

New job applications will be revamped so that every American can easily and freely designate "U.S. citizen" on his or her application. All other race designations will be reserved for foreign applicants, hired only after desirous qualified Americans have been given their choice of jobs.

From the President of the United States, to investigators, to the janitors in our prisons, all the way down to city hall - every employee will understand their job and do it efficiently. Every employee will understand that he or she works for and is paid by the good and hardworking citizens of this country, and that his or her function is to protect the rights of those citizens. Every employee will operate in the best interest of its citizenry. Every employee will follow directives instead of controlling and baby sitting, give instead of taking advantage, and enhance individual prosperity instead of competing for it. Every employee will perpetuate quality productivity, low overhead, training, a good work environment, fair and honest marketing techniques, and friendly courteous services from within their work places - all government offices throughout America and overseas.

We citizens will pay a good wage, provide good benefits, and never demand more than can reasonably be expected. But we'll be firm when we have to. From now on, when we ask for something, our government employees will say "Yes Ma'am or Yes Sir" in a language we can understand - English.

We'll put a freeze on all recently-approved pay increases, and immediately reduce present staff salaries and benefits to the level of the average American performing a similar service in the public sector. Holidays, a few personal days, and vacations equivalent to the private sector will be acceptable. And we want time cards punched. Loitering on the campaign trail will be considered an unexcused absence, and a day's wages will be deducted for every day of work missed. Twenty years of service will earn a fair pension, and those presently collecting who haven't given enough time will be cut off.

Government is costing American businesses and individuals too much, and forcing them to pay out in too many crazy directions. But with waste eliminated, we can reduce the costs and simplify the tax structure. Some kind of single flat tax will not only save millions in administrative costs, it will ensure we all pay our equal share. Prosperity will no longer be penalized. To spur more job creation, and enable the economy to move ever forward, we'll eliminate estate taxes, capital gains and similar savings and investment taxes. And we'll eradicate all the other little tax niches and unnecessary licensing fees that add up to the double and triple taxation that's forbidden by our Constitution.

Rush Limbaugh says we can make more "honest" money standing up for freedom than we can by opposing it - and we know he's proved it to be so. We heard him chuckle sarcastically when telling the story about the little Girl Scout who couldn't count the extra cookies she sold toward winning the prize, because a radio announcement gave her an unfair advantage. And we got his point.

We know that if we are to prosper and care for our needy, we need all the advantages. And our Constitution guarantees we have them. So we're trashing all these codes of ethics that unfairly stifle free enterprise in the Land of Opportunity. From now on, we're teaching our children how to take over as our successors and continue free enterprising until all the world succeeds.

From now on, we're combatting all those false indoctrinations that zap our strength and weaken our resolve- we're combatting them with a weapon called "truth." The next time somebody blames us for what they lack, we're reminding them that they are free to pursue happiness and prosperity only because we preserve freedom. We're reminding them that what they lack is not our fault, but that what they do not lack is because we are free to prosper and share. We will dedicate a fair portion of our strength to helping the incapable, and seeing that our charitable contributions reach the targeted needy. But because we know that no willing and able American lacks opportunity, we will have the courage to ignore those able bodies who are unwilling to carry their share of the load. We will insist on being the best we can be, and we will demand no less from those around us.

We will make our voices heard throughout the land. All it takes is some good old fashioned truth and common sense, coupled with a few flicks of our wrist and a little elbow grease, a few firm words spoken softly and in unison, supported by a few strokes from our heavy pens, a very few determined acts of defiance, a few less swipes with our credit cards, and a little more waving of our powerful economic sticks.

We will send our directives to each and every congressmen and senator at both the federal and state levels, to the President and every governor, to our local school boards, our city and county council members. We will respond to our local newspapers, television studios, and radio stations. We will attach our name and address to a note advising them of our cry - no, our demand for freedom. And we will do it in unison every day for as long as it takes to get our way.

We will emerge from the twenty-first century with a new attitude: one of renewed personal strength, social self respect and freedom - not fear, hesitation nor oppression. In the new millennium, we will be the best individuals we can be, living in the greatest nation on earth, passing freedom and prosperity on to our children - poised to truly bring the rest of the world along with us.

INDEX

A

Abortion 43, 64, 79, 92, 145
Administrative costs
        18, 94, 127, 157, 159
Affirmative action 39, 41–44, 68, 85,
        89, 90, 131, 150
Africa 22, 156
Agency(ies) 14, 37, 44, 64, 68, 69,
        95, 110, 117–119, 121, 124,
        125, 135, 140, 153,
Agent(s) 21, 57, 67–69, 76, 116–118,
        120, 122, 132, 151, 158
AIDS 11, 40, 41, 92, 96
American dream 13
American liberties 7
Animal-rights 11
Arafat, Yasir 49, 51
Atheist(s) 34–36
Attorney(s)
        64, 116, 118, 122, 124, 126, 137,
        138, 144

B

Bill of Rights 35
Birth control 92, 99
Bosnia 23, 48, 108
Bureaucrat 14, 15, 94, 138, 151
Bussing 29, 32, 88, 90, 92

C

Castro, Fidel 7, 48, 106
Chauvinism 37
Chemical warfare 17, 41
Child abuse 76, 77
Child care 91, 95, 101
China 17, 50, 57, 91, 108, 110
Christian(s) 35, 36, 49, 55, 145
Christian Coalition 33
Clinton, Bill
        22, 30, 31, 33, 49, 58, 65, 75–77,
        98, 99, 110, 116, 120, 161
CNN 103, 110, 112
Cold War 17
Columbia 56
Congress 9, 15, 35, 47, 56, 65, 90, 131
Congressman
        12, 52, 100, 105, 132, 136
Conservative 109, 111

Constitution
        22, 28, 31, 33, 35, 36, 65, 73,
        134, 135, 157, 159
Constitutional right 23, 33–35, 118,
        119, 131, 134, 148
Crime rate
        15, 17, 30, 56, 89, 130, 131, 133, 146, 148
Criminal(s) 11, 14, 16–18, 43, 48, 55,
        56, 59, 60, 63, 66, 69, 76, 100,
        122–127, 131–134, 137, 138,
        140–148
CSPAN 112
Cuba 48, 108

D

DARE 99
Death penalty 145
Democracy 6, 9, 13, 16, 38, 54, 107
Democrat 109
Diplomat 59
Discrimination 15, 34, 37, 42, 44
DNA testing 137
Dole, Bob 110
Drug(s)
        11, 15, 50, 56, 60, 63, 65, 66, 74, 75,
        79, 90, 96, 98, 99, 130, 131, 133
Drug pushers 56

E

Ebonics 30
Economy
        31, 32, 49, 50, 53, 56, 106, 151, 155, 159
Education 12, 28–30, 32, 40, 55, 88,
        89, 91, 94, 95, 97, 99, 101, 108,
        119, 143, 145
Elderly
        15, 38, 39, 42, 43, 58, 108, 123, 156
Emancipation Proclamation 38
English 31, 58, 159
Environment
        11, 13, 15, 16, 41, 57, 58, 107, 108,
        116–119, 130, 156, 157
EPA 117
Equal opportunity education 29
Euthanasia 145

F

FCC 121, 153
FDA 50
FDIC 153
Federal Reserve 152
Florida 55, 92, 115, 117, 124, 150
Florida Real Estate Commission
    (FREC) 124
Forefathers 18, 22, 31, 45, 100
Foreign policy 49, 52
Free press 105–107, 109, 113
Free society 10, 24, 39, 41, 45, 63, 138
Freedom fighters 16
Freedom of speech 35, 105

G

Gangs 130
Gangsters 64, 94
Ghetto 27–29, 89, 96, 130
Global economy 31, 32, 53
Gore, Al 57
Government control
    6, 8, 19, 29, 85, 99, 100, 107, 110,
    140, 156
Greenspan, Alan 152

H

Handicapped 15, 31, 38–40, 42, 43, 60,
    89, 92, 156
Hitler, Adolf 6, 8, 9
HIV 40, 93
Homosexual(s) 43
HRS 75, 76
Hussein, Saddam 7, 41

I

Illegal immigrant 11, 56–58
Immoral 63, 64
India 17, 156
Indoctrinae, (-ed), (-tion)
    6, 22, 23, 40, 51, 95, 110, 152, 160
Injustice 27, 34, 39, 126, 141
Iraq 23, 47, 48
IRS 59

J

Jackson, Jesse 22, 27, 30, 31
Johnson, Lyndon 9, 27, 30
Jones, Paula 67
Jury system 16, 140
Justice 13, 16, 17, 22, 52, 54, 59, 122,
    124–126, 137, 140, 141, 143–148
Juvenile 63, 65, 72

K

Kennedy, John F. 27
Khrushchev, Nikita 7, 8
King, Martin Luther 27
Kuwait 47, 48

L

Language 30–32, 42, 60, 98, 126,
    135, 148, 155, 159
Law enforcement
    57, 64, 69, 126, 133, 137, 140
Lawyer 64, 124–
    126, 138, 140, 143, 145, 150
Legislature (-ors), (-tion), (ing)
    64, 113, 127, 133
Lewinsky, Monica 111
Liberal 6, 107, 109, 111
Liberty 7, 17–19, 22, 42, 45, 51, 52,
    59, 105, 113, 135, 137, 157
Limbaugh, Rush 104, 111, 112, 159
Lobbyists 115

M

Malcolm X 28
McVeigh, Timothy 139, 145, 146
Media 24, 63, 99, 104–106, 109–112
Medicaid 152
Medicare 58, 152
Mexico 56, 110
Middle East 49, 57
Military 19, 47, 53, 54, 58, 64
Military draft 58
Militia 100
Minority 11, 27, 30, 36, 134
Moral code 11, 12, 15
Moral standards 73

N

National Association of Realtors (NAR)
    115
National Day of Prayer 65
National Education Association 29, 89
Nazi(s) 6, 90, 91, 111
NBC 105
NEA 15, 29, 30, 89, 92, 93, 99
Nuclear 15, 23, 41, 48–50, 92

O

Oppression 6, 8, 12, 14, 18, 19, 22,
    24, 35, 41, 59, 157, 161

P

Police
17, 71, 111, 124, 129, 131, 132, 137
Police brutality 25, 64
Politically incorrect 17
Poverty 8, 15, 19, 21, 22, 27–29, 32,
51, 68, 89, 156, 157
Pray(er) 12, 15, 33–35, 65, 78, 85, 109
Prejudice(d)
22, 23, 32, 33, 34, 37, 38, 42, 140
Press, the 18, 35, 66, 104–107, 109, 111,
112, 137
Private property rights
15, 18, 90, 115, 116, 134
Pro-choice 43, 92
Propaganda
14, 17, 34, 75, 79, 94, 111, 139, 150
Property owners 42, 119
Prosperity
17, 22, 24, 31, 48, 65, 100, 107–109,
116, 157–161
Public school 40, 55, 89, 92

R

Racial tension 21, 24
Racism 25, 29
Recycle (-ing) 16, 116, 149
Regulation (s)
14, 27, 37, 41, 42, 59, 64, 69, 115, 116
117, 121–124, 126, 127, 130, 131,
135, 137, 146, 148, 151, 152
Religion 17, 31, 33–37, 44, 65, 79, 97,
98, 145
Representatives, elected
16, 36, 47, 51, 56, 65, 67–69, 103,
109, 127, 135
Russia 17

S

Saudi Arabia 47, 48, 54
Scandal 63, 67, 112
School(s) 10, 12, 15, 17, 28–30, 33,
35, 37, 40, 41, 44, 50, 55–58,
60, 65, 67, 71, 73, 75, 78, 79, 82, 83,
87–89, 90, 92–96, 98–100, 123,
133, 147, 153, 156, 158, 161
Sex 73, 79, 92, 93, 96, 98, 99, 104, 106,
107, 110, 112, 122, 131, 148
Sex education 12, 92
Silent Majority 18
Simpson, O.J. 111, 122, 139, 140
Small business 11, 152
Smith, Susan 144
Social programs 15, 18, 32, 43

Social Security 38, 58, 151
Socialism 9, 18, 105, 151
Soldier(s) 49, 53, 54, 129
Strawberries, Mexican 50, 56, 67, 92

T

Tax(es) 8, 9, 18, 25, 27–29, 32, 38,
41, 58, 59, 67, 79, 89–91, 101,
103, 110, 115, 116, 119, 124, 127,
129–131, 136, 152, 157, 159
Taxpayer(s)
42, 50, 55, 93, 118, 145, 146,
148–152
Technology 11, 13
Teenager(s)
6, 11, 56, 72, 74, 78, 79, 84, 100, 122
Terrorism 49, 56, 57
Troops 28, 48, 54

U

Uncle Sam
17, 71, 96, 101, 106, 150, 154, 155, 158
United Nations 47–50, 53, 54
Utopia 16, 17, 19, 77, 156

V

Vietnam 8, 23, 47, 51
Violence 15, 28, 37, 44, 73, 79, 88–90, 93
Violence among the children 71

W

Wallace, George 28
Washington, D.C. 47, 52, 110, 115
Welfare
11, 55, 58, 60, 74, 91, 108, 130, 151, 153
Whitewater 66
Women's Suffrage 38
World Trade Center bombing 57

Y

Yeltsin, Boris 110